Tweed Rivers

Tweed Rivers

New writing and art inspired by
the rivers of the Tweed catchment

Edited by Ken Cockburn
and James Carter

platform projects
Luath Press Ltd
Tweed Rivers Interpretation Project
2005

Editorial Concept © TRIP, 2004
Text and Images © the authors and artists, 2005

Designed by StudioLR
Printed by J. Thomson Colour Printers
Edition of 2000 copies
Typeset in Stone Serif and Swiss 721

Published by:

platform projects
21A West Mayfield
Edinburgh EH9 1TQ
www.platformprojects.org

Luath Press Ltd
543/2 Castlehill
The Royal Mile
Edinburgh EH1 2ND
www.luath.co.uk

Tweed Rivers Interpretation Project
Scottish Borders Council
Planning and Economic Development
Newtown St Boswells TD6 0SA
www.scotborders.gov.uk

The Project is a partnership between Scottish Borders Council, Scottish Natural
Heritage, Scottish Borders Enterprise, Tweed Forum, Scottish Borders Tourist Board,
and Forest Enterprise.

The publishers acknowledge support from the Scottish Arts Council towards the
publication of this title.

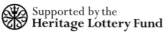

ISBN: 1-905222-25-4

Tweed Rivers

Preface

A raindrop falls on the crest of a hill. The way it rolls will take it through one river basin, or another; through one set of landscapes, stories and allegiances, or another.

River catchments are not always obvious, but they shape identity and forge connections in ways that transcend politics. From 1999 to 2005 the Tweed Rivers Interpretation Project has worked to celebrate the rivers that flow into Tweed and the land they define: this book is part of that project.

Interpretation here means encouraging people to explore, appreciate, and build their own relationship with a place. The Project has worked to bring alive the stories of various sites within the Tweed catchment, from viewpoints and Iron Age hill forts to eighteenth century follies and landmarks for local folk tales – you can find a list on pages 251–252. At many of them we used 'conventional' media to give some insight into the history, nature or culture of the place. At others, we have involved poets, sculptors and landscape designers to create site-specific work that we hope will offer alternative ways of thinking about the places concerned, and create lasting pieces that may become part of the area's heritage in their own right.

We were keen to extend this site-based work to give more freedom to a creative engagement with the rivers and their landscapes. This book is the result – a varied anthology that explores both the diversity of the rivers, and the richness of the cultural life around them. It is not a guidebook, nor a history: there are plenty of those already. Instead, we hope that it will be a companion as you explore these wonderful places, and after (or if) you leave, an evocation of them.

We invited proposals for contributions to the book in spring 2004, setting out the structure of a chapter dedicated to each of the main rivers, with each chapter the work of one writer and one visual artist.

We were pleased to receive over fifty submissions, featuring a range of artistic responses: poems, stories, essays and short prose; etchings, woodcuts, watercolours and acrylics; colour, black and white, and pinhole photography. Over the course of a long afternoon of debate and discussion, during which tempers showed remarkably few signs of fraying, we and Iain Macaulay, Arts Development

Officer at Scottish Borders Council, drew up a short leet. Among the visual proposals, there was very little documentary photography, and we decided to omit this approach as we felt that its realism, if featured only once or twice in the book, would be out of keeping with the more visually varied and 'interpreted' landscapes we were otherwise including.

Allocating rivers to authors and artists was a challenge: not all contributors were allocated their preferred stretch of water, nor indeed their preferred partner: we thank them for their patience and adaptability in accepting the commissions as offered. There was also, in the cases of those who arrived 'unpartnered', some matchmaking to do. We are pleased that all the artistic marriages we contracted have lasted long enough for the completion of the commission; some, we might hope, will continue once this book is completed.

The work, when we received it, was in some cases complete: text and images finalised and integrated. This makes the editor's job an easy one. In other cases, we received more work than we had space for, and had to make cuts; this is particularly true in the case of Katrina Porteous' long poem about the Tweed from which certain sections (indicated in the text by a row of asterisks) have been omitted for reasons of space. We hope that Katrina finds the opportunity to publish it in its entirety in the future. We also received submissions where the visuals and the text were not yet co-ordinated, and we undertook the task of ordering and matching ourselves.

Most of the work included here was made especially for this project, and is being published for the first time. One exception is the work on the River Teviot by John Murray and John McGregor; featured here are poems and images from a longer sequence called *Watermarks*, which has been widely exhibited, and which we are pleased to present here in book form for the first time.

There are many people we wish to thank for making this book possible, in particular all the contributors, all those who took the time and trouble to submit proposals in spring 2004, and the Project steering group who accepted the idea of producing a book that did not seem to conform to any easily understood standards! We also thank Cluny Sheeler of platform projects, Lucy Richards and all at StudioLR, Iain Macaulay at Scottish Borders Council, and Gavin MacDougall at Luath Press Ltd for their advice, support and encouragement; and E.V. Lucas, whose 1899 anthology *The Open Road – a little book for wayfarers* inspired this concept.

Ken Cockburn, platform projects
James Carter, Tweed Rivers Interpretation Project

Essay   **Up The Watters**
Words   **Gavin Bowd**

'Did ye see the Eclipse, on Monday?' asked a Selkirk man of his crony. 'Man, No! I was up the watters that day.' Which reply conveyed, perhaps not so much the feeling that an eclipse was a frivolous affair pertaining to geographically remote Selkirk alone, as that the answerer had been too deeply engaged up the waters with other business to have leisure to attend to such petty trifles as solar phenomena.

Andrew and John Lang, *Highways and Byways in the Border*

Despite being criminally overlooked by Ptolemy, the Tweed has, indeed, not been a place for petty trifles. Catchment brings enchantment, rivers rivalry. According to French phenomenologist Gaston Bachelard, 'water marks a poetic climate'. What follows here is an extremely partial geopoetic survey of that rough rectangle 'between Berwick and Bield'.

In 'The Borders', Hugh MacDiarmid rightly celebrates 'the combination o' the placid wi' the intense'. Let's begin with the intense. It was at Flodden, where Tweed meets Till, that independent Scotland died. At Fernihirst, bloodthirsty Scots bartered from French commander Sieur d'Essé a captured Spanish mercenary: 'They tied his hands and feet and head together, and placed him thus trussed in the middle of an open space, and ran upon him with their lances, until he was dead and his body hacked in a thousand pieces, which they divided among them and carried away on the iron points of their spears'. The waters pass beneath Manslaughter Law and the tomb of Field Marshal Haig, through Wedale, 'dale of woes', past the mysterious earthworks of The Catrail, to which, according to legend, the doomed tribe of Damnonii retreated after the disaster of the Battle of Degsastan, past war memorials to Gala lads massacred at Gallipoli and to herded shepherd boys of Yarrowford. Near the source of the Tweed, Talla reservoir now submerges the caves and cleughs where Covenanters lurked.

This region has been highly productive of that quintessential object of poetic reverie: the ruin. Thus, contemplating the derisory rubble of Roxburgh Castle, John Leyden exclaimed:

Fallen are thy towers, and where the palace stood
In glory grandeur waves your hanging wood;
Crushed are thy halls, save where the peasant sees
One moss-clad ruin rise between the trees.

Up the waters, there is an abundant trail of devastated and abandoned castles, keeps and abbeys. Massacre, rape, iconoclasm and pillage have amply served Apollo's lyre. Thomas the Rhymer does not seem to lie when he reports: 'a' the blude that's shed on earth/Rins through the springs of that cuntrie.'

Let's not forget the rebels: Merlin's last stand for paganism at Powsail Burn; or the bluster of the Outlaw Murray:

Thir lands of Ettrick Foreste fair,
I wan them from the enemie;
Like as I wan them, sae will I keep them,
Contrair a' kings in Christentie.

MacDiarmid ejaculates: 'this bolshevik bog suits me doon tae the grun'!'

But violence here does not simply involve worldly nations, tribes and creeds. This is a glamour-haunted land. The valleys ring with the bridle bells of fairy-troopers as well as moss-troopers. There is a constant fear of abduction, of elf-attack: the ballads of True Thomas, Young Tamlane and Kilmeny teach us to be on our guard. The Victorian *schloss* of Glenmayne almost tempted Michael Jackson from Neverland ... And there is always the kelpie, sulking and dripping nearby, ready to lure us to a liquid grave. The Tweed catchment may lack its Edgar Allan Poe, but it has shown examples of what Bachelard calls the 'Ophelia complex', of how water is 'the element of the young and beautiful death'. Think of the dead callant in the 'Dowie Dens of Yarrow', his lover kissing his wounds until her lips are red. Think also of those two girls drowned in Eden when a miller closed his sluice.

There is space also for the tragi-comic: the last Ker of Littledean, emerging from his castle one fine morning, unusually dressed in a sleeping gown, only to be gored to death by his favourite bull, who had understandably failed to recognise him;

or that time in 1895, when the Tweed froze up at Stobo and, before the curlers would play their 'roaring game', all the bachelors of the area were rounded up to test the ice.

But it would be wrong to associate the Tweed catchment only with violence. No ancient weapon has ever been found in the river, nor at The Catrail, further deepening its enigma. At Newstead were exhumed helmets in the shape of heads of pretty Greek girls, and enamelled brooches of native women who dwelt with Roman lovers. John Buchan wrote: 'if Paradise be a renewal of what was happy and innocent in our earthly days, mine will be some golden afternoon within sight and sound of Tweed.' On his pilgrimage to Abbotsford in 1858, the German Theodor Fontane noted: 'Nowhere is there any striking beauty, but everywhere a smiling grace and the mild hand of civilisation, which seems to strike one like the west wind.'

One of this area's most extravagant eulogists was Professor John Veitch (1829–94), who abandoned Logic to pen *The History and Poetry of the Scottish Border*. For Veitch, the peculiar course of the Tweed 'represents a wavy line of force steadily pursuing its way to an end or point. The confluent streams of north-west and south-east unite in harmony in its peaceful valley, and murmur in one full flow along its green hillsides and through its tranquil haughs – a fitting boundary-line between the old hostile kingdoms – the opposing forces of north and south'. The Professor does not avoid the violence that seethes in the ballads, and sees in the changing moods of the landscape an echo of human history. But his *History* argues for a growing 'Nature-feeling' in Borders poetry. After 'long, dark years of mortal strife', the hard heart is softened by waters running across a Silurian ground-frame. Towards the end of his own opus, 'The Tweed', he announces:

> *A kindlier spirit now has grown within*
> *The heart of man, – by Nature part inspired,*
> *And part to Nature given by the soul.*
> *The awesome forest dark is now with love illumed.*

Despite its low-velocity flow, its relative lack of commercial and geopolitical importance – *pace* Veitch, the Tweed waters have rarely marked a national frontier – or perhaps because of all this, the Tweed and its tributaries have inspired declarations of love that combine the local and the global. At Berwick, George Borrow's Lavengro bursts into tears and says: 'neither the stately Danube, nor the beauteous Rhine, with all their fame, though abundant, needst thou envy, thou pure island stream!' That lyrical lush Robert Fergusson dares to assert:

> *On Leader Haughs and Yarrow Braes,*
> *Arcadia herds wad tyne their lays,*
> *To hear the mair melodious sounds*
> *That live on our poetic grounds.*

MacDiarmid is not afraid to claim:

> *The Volga, the Danube, the Thames,*
> *The Mississippi are mighty waterways.*
> *Beside them Yarrow's but a wee burn*
> *Yet ootranks them in its poets' lays.*

These waters have been close to the hearts of doomed boyfriends of the Muse: Robert Crawford drowning on his way back from France; Thomas Pringle, author of *Afar in the Desert*, returning in disgust from the Kaffir border; John Leyden publishing *Scenes of Infancy* while dying in Java; Mungo Park leaving Walter Scott at the Tweed before the Niger consumed him; and the ailing Scott changing 'Green Eildon-hill and Cheviot/For warm Vesuvio's vine-clad slopes' (Wordsworth).

But there can be something annoying about this 'feeling for Nature' in Borders poetry. Is it not, to borrow the American culture critic Fredric Jameson's phrase, 'the symbolic resolution of intolerable social contradiction'? Does it not seek to escape an undeniable reality: the economy, stupid? In 1666, the last wandering Border minstrel, Burne the Violer, played Scotch tunes to Samuel Pepys in Lord Lauderdale's house; also in that year, a Weavers' Corporation was established in Galashiels and the Privy Council complied with the application from one Philip Van den Straaten, native of Bruges, for the dressing and refining of wool in Kelso. 1789 was bliss for the young Wordsworth, but also for Robert Walker of Galashiels, who was awarded a grant by the Board of Manufactures towards the purchase of a spinning-jenny. Sheep-drainage gets little mention in the pentameters of the early nineteenth century. While Fontane pays his respects to the 'healthy romanticism' of Abbotsford, his compatriot, Karl Marx, is citing the Lowland farmer as an example of the 'metamorphoses of capital and their circuit'.

Partisans of the 'feeling for Nature' are wont to protest against development. Veitch contrasts Border poetry with 'literary manufactures'. When the last Douglas of Queensberry turned to timber production at Neidpath, Wordsworth, who had long since given up on Revolution, protested in solidarity with 'a brotherhood of venerable trees'. The depths of bourgeois hypocrisy were plumbed by one 'J.B. Selkirk', *nom de plume* of a wool manufacturer, who dared to write, in 'The Vale of Ettrick Past and Present':

> *The Forest's gone! the world's improved since then!*
> *A forest now of chimneys, Babel-high,*
> *Belch out their blackened breath against the sky.*
> *Take off your hats to Progress, gentlemen!*
> *So runs the world; but as for me, heigh-ho!*
> *I should have lived four hundred years ago.*

These lines were written in the 'Yarrow Villa' in ... Cannes. No wonder the Tweedies 'delaittit in the slaughter of David Riccio'.

There emerges a conflict between a certain type of poetry and the landscape it claims to celebrate. Galashiels is a classic example. Arguably the birthplace of the Scottish Industrial Revolution, this town owes its wealth and identity to the water running through it. In 1898, Robert Hall asserted: 'As a town, it is the architect of its own fortunes, owing its birth and progress to the energy and perseverance of the men who planted their spinning mills on the banks of the Gala, discerning the value of the power possessed by that classic stream.' A few years previous, had the Japanese ambassador not visited such factories and joined local worthies at the Mill Lade in a toast to the Mikado? Among all the common ridings, Galashiels is the only one to define itself aquatically, singing the superiority of the Braw Lads of Gala Water over those of Yarrow Braes and Ettrick Shaws. In another song, 'On the banks o' Gala

Water/There grows a flower so fair/Blooming forth in tender beauty'. It is poignant that, in the 1970s, one Braw Lad made the ultimate sacrifice while fording Tweed.

But growing wealth and population did not please the Late Romantic poet. Andrew and John Lang were scandalised to see a dead pig floating outside the Technical College. They were blind to the exotic flowers that flourished briefly by those waters. They had obviously not read this Baudelairean passage from Ida Hayward: 'As one investigates the subject more closely it is an extraordinary chapter in plant history that is unrolled even as one stands within sight of Melrose and Abbotsford. One sees many a distant port and the ships lading their wool cargoes; the magnificent entrance to Cape Town dominated by Table Mountain, an outpost of the illimitable veldt spangled with bright composites, Helichrysum, tiny Cotula and discoid Matricarias; the busy Rue de Cannebière, itself named from the Alien Hemp, leading to La Joliette, whence sailed Massilia's triremes, and to which came the early Phoenician voyagers.'

It was the Tramp Poet, Roger Quin (1850–1925), who most perversely and movingly resisted the real. Dividing his time between Glasgow, where people suffered 'on the very borderland of being', and Galashiels and its environs, he contrasted urban hell with pastoral heaven. In 'The Borderland' he writes:

> From the moorland and the meadows
> To this City of the Shadows,
> Where I wander old and lonely, comes the call I understand;
> In clear, soft tones enthralling,
> It is calling, calling, calling –
> 'Tis the Spirit of the Open from that dear old Borderland.

At the top of Barr Road, you will find a plaque to Roger Quin, who 'gazed on Scotland's Eden from the spur of Gala Hill'. His vista includes Abbotsford, Melrose Abbey and the Eildons. Due to a quirk in the hillside, Galashiels is hidden.

The flow of Tweed catchment poetry seems to have more or less dried up since then. Hugh MacDiarmid only wrote 'The Borders', and was much more of an Esk man. In 1938, Virginia Woolf visited Galashiels, described it in one word,

'Hideous', then killed herself. In 'On the Border', Kenneth White's motif is 'rough wind, a rock and a rowan tree': streamlets do not smooth the Hyperborean hard man. The air and water have been purified, the circuit of capital has changed its course, the last mill in the Gala Valley specialises in... finishing. We live in a post-industrial landscape where, in the words of Mark E Smith, 'the valley rings with ice cream vans'. But poets sensitive to Nature have not returned with the trout and salmon. Although in 1992, in pure Veitchean style, one Ian Bavington Jones portrayed the Tweed as 'that wild and beautiful region which somehow combines the remoteness of Scottish upland scenery with the pastoral, almost Arcadian qualities of the English landscape.'

It is not that the modern Tweed is without drama. Flying high over the landscapes of South America, Le Corbusier developed his *law of the meander*, remarking: 'the course of these rivers demonstrates peacefully the inevitable consequences of the laws of physics'. The modernist architect could often get things wrong. Think of that glorious night of the 12th August 1948. According to *The Meteorological Magazine*, a spiralled occlusion with a warm tongue over and east of it, and a large cold tongue to the south-west of it, an ageostrophic wind, a dying low from Iceland and a large orographic effect combined, exceptionally, to drop 400 million tons of water on the Tweed catchment. It was the worst flood since 1294. The waters reached points beyond any previous level recorded, burns became rivers for a day, some changed course, sweeping away houses, bridges and livestock, tidal banks built by Napoleonic prisoners, disrupting even swimming-club competitions. Then, we learn, 'it degenerated to a trough in the circulation of a new system over Poland and moved south.' This hydrological carnival still awaits its poet.

In the meantime, let Bards meditate on these lines from 'The Young Tamlane':

> *Poetic fields encompass us around,*
> *And still we seem to tread on classic ground.*

Select Bibliography

Gaston Bachelard, *L'Eau et les rêves: essai sur l'imagination de la matière* (1947).

Anne Bell (ed), *The Diaries of Virginia Woolf Vol 5 1936–1941* (1985).

George Borrow, *Lavengro* (1851).

John Buchan, *Memory Hold-the-Door* (1940).

George Burnett, *Companion to Tweed* (1938).

T. Craig Brown, *The History of Selkirkshire* (1886).

Theodor Fontane, *Beyond the Tweed. A Tour of Scotland in 1858* (1998).

J. Glasspoole, 'Tweed Valley Floods. Heavy Rainfall of August 11–12 1948', *The Meteorological Magazine*, vol. 78 (1949), pp. 3–11.

Robert Hall, *The History of Galashiels* (1898).

Harrison, Pile and Thrift (eds.), *Patterned Ground. Entanglements of Nature and Culture* (2004).

Fredric Jameson, *The Political Unconscious. Narrative as a Socially Symbolic Act* (1981).

Andrew and John Lang, *Highways and Byways in the Border* (1913).

Hugh MacDiarmid, *Complete Poems Volume 2* (1994).

Roger Quin, *The Borderland and other poems* (1930).

J. B. Selkirk, *Songs of Yarrow and The Border* (1896).

John Veitch, *The History and Poetry of The Scottish Borders* (1893).

John Veitch, *The Tweed* (1875).

Kenneth White, *Collected Poems* (2003).

River   Tweed: Source – Peebles
Words   Katrina Porteous
Images   Susheila Jamieson

On the scarred hill, a house with no road.
The burn cuts the brae as an axe pares wood.
The shepherd of Earlshaugh in his tacketty boots
Has set out over the hill without a word.

Dense walls of forest have enfolded him;
Dark crowds of promises. He is swallowed up
With the thieves' road, the Roman road, the iron-age scatterings.
The black trees bleed the valley, drop by drop.

Small mutterings. The restlessness of water. Nothing certain
But its movement and the earth's response. The Powskein; the Corr.
The hills hold the memory of ice and rain. Each hollow
Deepens by the year,

Until there is no house, no road, no miles of forest,
Only the whispering roads of water. Oily, black,
Oozing from mud, glaur, rashers, Tweed begins to murmur·
Never look back.

Peat-red,
Keel-red,
Blood-shot,
Dark at the root,

Down
       it slips,

Last year's pale stalks
Dipping their fingers
In its bitter water.

A hush. A secret.
The first of many meetings.

In the freshest of voices
The oldest of songs

Ripples among Palaeozoic stones,
By boulders, furry as animals,

Among islands of elephantine butterbur,
In deep, slow tributes of golden coins,

Where, like the shadows of the grass, quick as sparks,
Black swarf, flying to the magnet or away from it
In sudden, thrilling rushes, under the water's wrinkled skin,
Salmon parr obey a far-off music.

        * * *

Under a roof of ash and sycamore
The dipper curtseys.

The wagtail somersaults,
Light as a gnat.

Between rocky banks,
Green, deep, glassy,
Tweed slides –

Speeds –

And tumbles, torn –
Teems down the linn,
Dives, white spurts
Gushing, leaping,
Drops of spun glass –
Goes over in shreds,
Threads,

A silver loom-warp.

Fresh!

And under the echoing arch,
Trapped in the coign,
A white, whirling galaxy
Circles and circles,

Endlessly chasing its tail.

Millstone. Altarstone.
Stone of lost stories:
When does a burn
Become a river?

When does a people
Forget where it came from?
Hearthstone, whetstone,
Peel and bale-fire.

Stony stillness.
The whisper of water,
The endless turning
Of the sky's grey mill:

Who killed Merlin?
The shepherds of Drumelzier
By the bark-brown water
Under Rachan Hill.

　　　* * *

Peaceful, worn deep by the long grind,
The steep, solemn valley, filling with pine, oak, ash –
Layer on green layer, rounded as summer cloud-banks –
Cradles the young river in its curves;

And, sinuously, through the ringing leaves –
Blackbird, song-thrush, echoing ever more distant –
Tweed, intent on the future, gathers its forces,

Under the shadowy embrace of seven arches,
Under the dark frown of Neidpath, sprung from the whin,

The blood of two hatreds fused in one green vein.

River	**Lyne Water**
Words	**Valerie Gillies**
Images	**John Rogers**

The Cauld Stane Slap

The pass in the gap
    a break in the cloud
skylarks spark up
    wing-beats aloud

all set each other going
    barred and crested rise
flying and singing
    from the cup of surprise

at the outburst of the spring
    their bubbling song soars
every moment beginning
    the voice of the source

Ravendean Burn

Just knowing he's out there is enough.
A far-away bird flies with the black clouds.

Then a noise like no other you'll ever hear:
a throat-singer from the steppes, a pig-snort,

a starburst, a log-pile rolling, cork-drawing pops,
body-blow drums, horses' hooves on a hard road.

This is sooo raven. He comes cronking over
to speak to you. He likes to toc the toc.

Anything with a vocal edge goes down well
with him. *Prruk prruk. Krroak krronk.*

Toc toc toc. Corvus corax corax. Corbie –
quirky breakbeats all the way, gruff barks.

The ravens are returning to Ravendean,
the black one roosts on White Craig,

new birds on the ancestral crag. He feeds
the young ravens who cry out to him.

The Roman augurs would be prophesying
with these cries of *korp korp* from his axe-bill.

He's sporting his thunderhead today, sings
his raven-praise of storm-winds, flips over

till he flies upside-down, turns iridescent,
now beats his direct flight into the distant hills.

Lynedale

William Keyden (1768–1826) the Laird of Lynedale wanted to be
buried in his own garden on the banks of the Lyne. His wish was ignored.

Crooked Jock will let
      the river off the hook
down to Lynedale next
      – stay and look –

hawthorn and briarbush
      on the brow of the mound
the laird's last wish
      for his garden ground

he'd push up the daisies
      from his grassy pillow
touched by the breeze
      over rock and billow

his wish never granted
      who can say
if the dell is haunted
      he's here to stay

the glade is his own
      with a sunbeam in it
where his green crown
      opens on the infinite

Rumblin Tam

Try finding Rumblin Tam, take the flight
Of steps leading down to his grotto in the shade.
Campers come to fill their bottles, look for light.
Drinkers add this water to their whisky.
You'll hear him first, a run of sound, a drone,
A pounding pulse, a thumping heartbeat.
Pipes give the spring a voice of his own
To throb from the stones beneath your feet.

Put your ear to the drum of old masonry
And hear his deep bass plumb the mysteries.
The waters play through Rumblin Tam to rout
And sound the conch and tap and spout
– a half penny per glass on market day –
The clear silver streamer he waves away.

Old Romanno Bridge

A melancholy thistle	with	big flower heads
a corbelled string-course	above	the single arch
springing over	the stream	two flood-arches
on the left bank	above	marshy channels
There's nowhere	on earth	we cannot go
we just have	to cross	the bridge

Romanno Terraces

The drag and drop of step-like terraces
Write lines to us in wintry black on white
With their steep risers and narrow treads,
Ribbed slits and scoops of light.

Early cultivation is a line of cut,
A row of turf-seats, grassy scalps,
A slice of this slope raised up
Tiny field by field, alp by alp.

Their flight of steps, time's escalator
On the face of a hill with an outward curve.
Come down, come down, ancestors, spectators
Watching us, we know when we're observed,
Our children are getting used to going away,
The future will arrive unexpectedly.

Hell's Cleugh

Rive o the wunds   up the wrang close
canyon o nicht   an crack o doom
on the laigh road   tae *l'infernaccio*

the ill place   in a hause-pipe
Satan's gullet   auld clootie's clint
hell's mou   earl o hell's swallie

daith's doonfa   clift o the fient
scaur o hades   in the shaddow half
the mirkness   o muckle hell

hird o Hell's Cleuch   look aboot ye
deil ye dae   or dinnae dae
it's no for nocht   the corbie craws

Newlands

The river deepens here, glides silently by venerable trees
and simple roofless church. Take shelter from the storm
under the first round-headed doorway, kin to a rainbow.

The door through which you see the south is opening onto
distance unfolding, to rain moving over the Ladyurd hills
and far Penveny. Everything radiates outwards from here,

from this gate of heaven, a door of blessings upon earth,
the true doorway shows creation to the living,
the temple door is opening of its own accord.

Drochil Castle

A marksman's eye, a glint at the gun-loop
in the tower. Flanking fire,
a trick of moonlight, a ghost
with ruffles and a sword runs
then pauses to look back up
at the carved heart and the fetterlock
sign of the warden of the borders.
The initials over the window
of the west front: ID for James Douglas
Earl of Morton, first bridegroom to be
beheaded by his own iron Maiden.

Harehope Rings

haring up to Harehope Rings

Lyne and Happrew

The river makes a horseshoe bend and then
two horses lift their heads from opposite banks.

On the left, from Lyne, is the grey racing mare,
a sprinter with her explosive turn of hoof,
a dancer, a looker, a stormer, a winner.
If you saw her in the morning gallops
you'd think Pegasus himself couldn't catch her.
If you want to ride her, on you go,
but we may not see you for a while!

On the right, from Easter Happrew, a horse-head
in greenish bronze shows up at this moment
after two thousand years, from harness trappings
reined in by a tribe of skilful drivers. The marks
of his soft collar, strap and buckle. Look
between his neat ears, over his rough mane
towards the turf ramparts of the perfect fort
and see the same hills on the move now,
horses and chariots emerging from the mist,
with every jolt the wheels spin dangerously close.

That unknown place, name of *Carbantorigon*,
must be here somewhere ...

Beggarpath Bridge

eftir Kikaku

bridge at dayligaun
a thoosan haunds
skiff the caipstane

Sangam

Land between two rivers
narrows to a fine point
a spit, a heron's bill

it's some spate –
pulses of heavy rain all day
steam rising off the rivers

hanging in a haze
above the racing waters
Lyne is higher, backing off

from red Tweed, cream crests
of big waves sweep downstream
in the universal deluge

walk towards the meeting
saying all the names
of the Ganges, *matritamah*

most maternal
today the world-river's life
is flowing through every river

The Lyne Valley

We will gather now from side valleys and hopes
bare of trees, drink from every burn-mouth,
wear our ring-fort crowns above hill-slopes.
The river runs through all we do. Linton children out
playing freely on the green, splash in the shallows.
Our mustering-grounds are water-margins, jointed rush.
Three children's long cist-graves on a gravel knoll
fill with wild grasses. Line, Lin, Lyne names us.

Uplands where blackface ewes are split into hefts
and summered on the hill. Wind-clipped mats
of heather at the summits. Meander, snaky beast,
our glistening body of water. Lyne cuts south-east
across old Silurian rocks in an undersea dream.
We see Tweed capture a more ancient stream.

River Leithen Water
Words Dorothy Alexander
Images Mary Kenny

CONFLICT

TRADE

SURVIVE

Life is Sweet

She liked to eat trout with her fingers, with only a sprinkling of salt as accompaniment. The skin slid off easily. It was soft but crisp with its coating of fried oatmeal. The flesh was creamy white with a layer of the softest grey-brown where it attached to the darker skin of the body. Its sweetness mixed with the dustiness of the oatmeal. It tasted of the smell of the river; a taste that had an undertone of something flat and mudded and still, that if it was too strong she called 'fresh', and did not like. The flesh was easy to pull off the bones. The bones were opaque, except sometimes, where the flesh was deep and not completely cooked, they were translucent, and blood, still red, adhered.

To catch a fish you need a fly. To make a fly you wind coloured silks and feathers around small metal hooks.

She loved watching her father tie flies. He would sit in his chair beside the window surrounded by reels of coloured thread, boxes of hooks of different sizes, hackle pliers, scissors, tweezers, a needle stuck in a piece of wood, a lump of beeswax lined with grooves where countless threads had been pulled across it to waterproof them, bottles of old nail varnish, scraps of fine gold and silver braid, gold wire, the iridescent neck feathers of a cock pheasant, the remains of an old feather hat, and a hen pheasant's wing, stiff and dry. One single feather, trimmed and slicked downward with the pull of a moistened thumb and forefinger, wound round a hook and fluffed out with the needle, then tied in with the most delicate of knots in the coloured thread and dabbed with varnish made a fly. They slid around and caught together in a small tin box.

Her father and grandfather knew where the fish were, facing upstream in the shelter of big stones, in the hollows of the riverbed, in the quieter eddies where the force of the main stream unravelled. They cast their lines out and over the water, out and over, tempting the fish with their hooks dressed up as flies. Their favourites were called March Brown and Greenwell's Glory. Sometimes they tried out homemade patterns made up as experiments. There always seemed to be one that the fish would take in preference on any given day. And when a fish took the fly, they would run it, let it tire itself out as it tried to get away, play the line out, reel it in, closer and closer, stumbling on the banking when concentration did not notice the uneven ground, patient, the rod bending to the pull of the fish, playing it into the shallows, the whisk of its belly dull white and flailing. They would guide it into the net and lift it onto the banking or onto stones at the side of the water, unhook it, bang it on the head and slide it into their bag, admiring it for a second or two, longer if it was a big one.

They worked in the mill, in the carding department. She knew all about carding. She had done a project at school. It's title was 'Wool Project'. She had done a rather good drawing of a blackface sheep that took up the whole of the front cover. Her writing was very neat. On one page there was a diagram of a carding machine which her father had drawn. Beneath this was a thicker piece of paper with examples of carding wire stuck on: bent metal pins of varying length, very fine, attached to bonded and felted material that covered the different sized rollers of the machine. The page opposite was blank as the wires would have damaged anything pasted there. She liked to run her finger along them. In one direction they felt smooth, but the slightest movement in the opposite direction and they dug into the skin of her fingers in such a way that movement was stopped dead and tiny indentations appeared at the tips of her fingers.

The carding machines teased out the raw, washed and dyed wool into a billowy mass that they then rolled into long slivers ready for spinning. The slivers were soft and broke easily. She had pasted in a picture of heavy machinery. A man stood at the side of it. His hands, as they busied in about the strands of wool, looked very small and white.

Her father and grandfather put the freshly caught trout into clear polythene bags. At the end of a day's fishing they would present the bags to her, her mother and her grandmother, display them, spread the fish out so that they could see how many were inside, what size they were. The bigger ones would be singled out for special attention. There would be speculation as to how many pounds each weighed. The fish were wet with river water and with the slimy fluids that came off and out of them. They slipped about beside one another, pushed against the polythene by their own

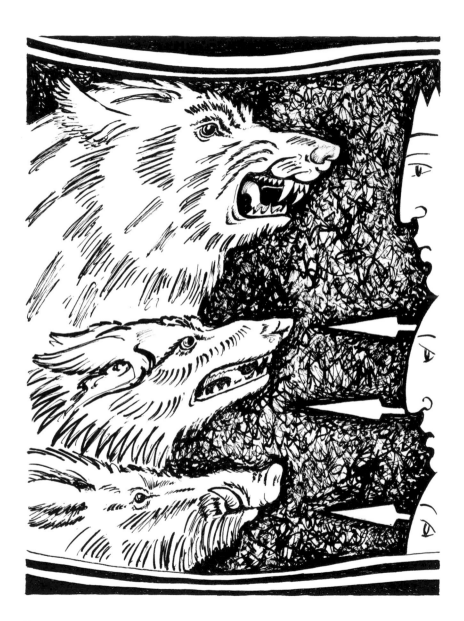

extinct

hunt

fish

weight, their plumpness making the bags bulge. The liquid surface of their dead eyes looked dull. Their skins were black-grey, brightening through pink and rainbow speckles to white, a creamy soft white that made the smear of blood that always settled in the bottom of the bags visible.

Her father took the basin out of the sink and laid it aside. He set the cold tap running. He got a sharp knife and the kitchen scissors out of the drawer. The bag of fish lay on the bunker. He spilled them into the sink and grabbed one.

'You need to get a good hold of them, they're slippy.'

He ran it under the tap to get rid of some of the slippery fluid.

'Okay? Get the sharp knife and scrape the scales off. Hold it by the tail, because you have to scrape up towards the head, like this.'

He rasped the knife up the side of the trout's body. The scales were see-through and lenticular. They floated on the water that ran across the bottom of the sink. He flipped the fish over and did the same on the other side.

'Then get the scissors and cut off the fins and tail, and then, get a good hold of it here,' he grasped it firmly round the middle, '... and cut off the head, behind the gills.'

She saw a pale and delicate frill as he opened one up for her.

'You'll usually manage it with the scissors, but sometimes, if its big, you'll need a knife.'

He needed to put a lot of pressure on the scissors.

'And then all you to do is this. See this wee hole here, put the knife or your scissors in there and slit it right up the belly.'

He did this and the guts spilled out.

'Then just get your thumb in and push it all out. Give it a good run under the tap to get rid of all the wee bloody bits, and there you go, one trout.'

The fish was slippery and firm. She had to pin it to the bottom of the sink with one hand while she scraped the scales off. They flew in all directions. Some landed on her arm. They felt light and plasticky. She rinsed them off under the tap. The scissors crunched through the fins and tail. The tail was extra crunchy because of the last remnant of the spine. She had to open the scissors extra wide to cut the head off. Her hand slipped with the effort. The handle of the scissors dug into the base of her thumb. But the slit up the belly was easy; the flesh was thin there and opened up like silk. There was something satisfying about the evacuation of the guts, a getting rid, as if the colours were wrong, the dark reds and crimsons and yellow oranges too vivid. The trout on the plate lay speckled and dark and rainbow and cream-white and silver: colours that made them hard to see against the bed of the stream, in the depths of a pool, in the broken light of the river as it tumbled over stones.

* * *

If this was a film the figures of her father and grandfather would appear in sepia tones, their silhouettes the archetypal silhouette and symbol of the fisherman. There would be a tree and a fence and hills in the background. She would introduce the film by saying that every year of her childhood, from April to September, her father and grandfather went fishing for trout. They fished the Tweed, the Manor, the Lyne, the Leithen, and on hot summer Sundays they would drive across the Paddy Slacks to Megget. On these days the whole family would go with them. They would picnic in the shelter of a red barn.

And as the images took on colour and began to move, she would tell how this was the story of her very short career as an angler, ended as it began at ten years of age. The sounds of the summer countryside, the nylon hiss of the line and mechanical spin of the reel would increase in volume through air sunthick and hazy with myriad particles of scuffed mud, pollen and airblown seedheads, while underneath it all the sound of the water, constant, busy, rushing, its energy pushing headlong and singing, would reverberate like so many voices. The camera would pan in on the brown rippling and flowing water as it caught the sun. Flashes of light would sparkle like golden stars. She'd be nine in this shot, roaming the banks of the Leithen just upstream from a flat, wide piece of grass where it was easy to park the car, finding flat stones to skim, scrabbling over drifts of loose river stones, coggling on them,

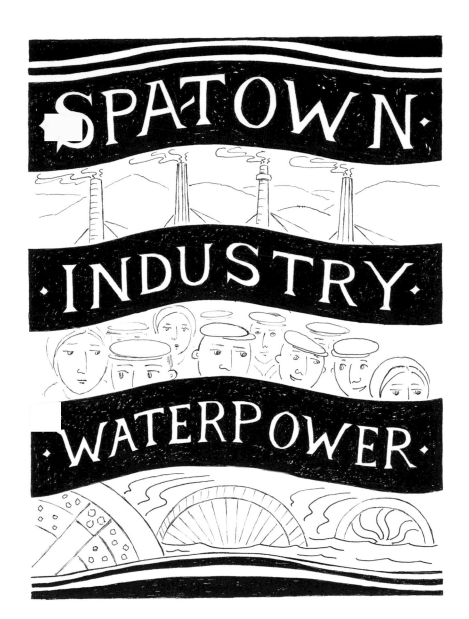

trying not to stand on sheep muck that was everywhere, watching her father and grandfather fish, being quiet and not skimming stones anywhere near them, listening to sheep munching and ripping the grass, the hills all around green and purple and gold, Lee Pen with its blot of trees at the foot, in shadow. There would be tenderness in her voice, but not the thoughtless tenderness of nostalgia. It might look as if her memories were bathed in an obscuring haze but it was just that they happened in summer evening sunshine, which *is* warm and golden and has within it that bittersweet longing that knows that such perfection must fade but wants to hold onto it. The reality of her memory was bittersweet. The mill was being taken over. Her grandfather's conversations had worry in them. They might lose their jobs. Her father did. Yet looking back all she could see was a happy child, loved and cared for, who knew somewhere inside herself that life is sweet. And that's not nostalgia; that's gratitude and fact and something to rejoice in.

And then there might be a time-lapse sequence of leaf fall, snow and the appearance of green shoots, because in the next shot she would be ten with her own rod, her father standing behind her, his hands on hers, pulling her arms back and flinging them forward to cast the line out and across, out and across the water, stretching and watching as the fly danced across the surface of the water, stretching and waiting, the evening sun radiating the smell of grass, sheep and river. The main narrative would start here, as she tried all by herself to cast the line: once, twice, thrice.

    The fly caught on something behind her. Her father sprang across to where it was tangled in the purple remnant of a thistle head, and released it with great delicacy so as not to snag his finger. She worked her way quietly along the bank, concentrating, casting, trying to get her fly to land over the invisible fish, feeling the whip of the rod, the hypnotic swish of the line as it rhythmed out on its teasing curve, getting caught in the opposite banking. Her grandfather waded across to free it.

    Then it happened. There was a tug on the line and she felt the pull of a fish, energy and struggle, and a feeling of weightlessness as she drew in the slack. She shouted. Her father put his rod down.

    'Keep a hold of it … That's right, wind it in.'

He was beside her, telling her when to pull and when to reel and when to let it out a bit, his hands enclosing hers. She could see the fish now. The white glint of its belly as it moved towards her, the pink of its mouth. It switched and twisted. She pulled it nearer and nearer. It would stop flailing for a few seconds, then, revived, beat the water with its flip flap muscular body. Her grandfather waded up to them. He had his net ready.

'Nice and steady. Just keep it steady.'

He manoeuvred the net in behind the fish, and there it was, lifted up and out of the water and set on the stones.

Movement, it was all movement. Flail, lash and twist, gasp, flail, lash, twist, gasp; all verb, alive, all life.

Her father held it with one hand as he worked the hook out of its mouth; its mouth open, gasping pink and white, cartilaginous, the hook rasped out of it.

'Come on then, you do it. It's your fish.'

Splash marks on the stones darkened the dry river mud. It rubbed off on the trout's body. She felt the gritty dust of it in her hand as she caught hold of its body. It was so very much alive. She had to hold it very tight.

'Look, there's a big stone. Lay it flat on that.'

He handed her a small metal cosh. It was heavy in her hand.

'One good thump, that's the best way.'

She moved the fish the short distance to the big flat stone. It wriggled and flailed less now. It lay quiet for short whiles when only its mouth would open and close as it gasped. No sound came out of it. Its tail flapped. She raised the cosh, aware of how its eye looked like water. Its eye like water while behind her silent fish that were speckled and dark and rainbow and cream-white and silver lay watchful in the broken light of the Leithen as it sang and hurried and tumbled over stones.

Cleikum Community home.

River Ettrick Water and Yarrow Water
Words Walter Elliot
Images Fred Cannon

A Song For Yarrow

A song for Yarrow. How to start?
It must be written from the heart,
And how to tell in one short tale
The story of the Yarrow vale?

An ancient minstrel, so they tell
Did sing the song of Yarrow well.
Faint echoes of his songs still last
To tell the tale of Yarrow's past.

The minstrel now is gone; but still,
When summer lights the Tinnes Hill
And heather blooms on Newark's braes
The ear can sense his ancient lays
For Yarrow as it rolls along
Still carries on the minstrel's song.

St Mary's Loch and Tibbie Shiel's Inn

As Wordsworth might have written if he were alive today

When first I saw fair Yarrow's stream
Some Minstrel's harp did seek my ear;
I stood as in a waking dream
While breathing in the air so clear.
For at my feet, St Mary's Lake
Did seem a land of bliss.
My heart was light as eyes did take
A scene so fair as this.

And could this be the famous vale?
The vale of so much sorrow
Where ancient minstrels tell the tale
The Dowie Dens of Yarrow.
It cannot be, for I must think
By no imagination
Could bloody ballad ever link
With this divine creation.

A cosy cottage nestles near,
A place of quiet reflection,
A place where one can sit and steer
The mind to recollection.
The blue skies, bright above the Lake
The hills reflected glory.
At Tibbie Shiel's, my ease I take
And here I end my story.

The Yarrow Churchyard

A shaft of strong sunlight breaks through the boughs
of the old twisted trees, creating moving patterns
of light and near darkness upon the short bleached grass;
a wavering chessboard in which the gravestones stand
like pieces ready for the master's hand.

Some are obviously king and queen pieces; many are pawns
while others are merely stones from the river,
wanting the dignity of initials even.

Does their size mirror the crumbled dust beneath?
Lichen, grey and yellow, colours the older stones.
Is the yellow lichen symbolic of a wealthier dust?
No one knows.

Neither are we privileged to know the dreams and fears
buried here. Was Walter Scott proud of the sharing a name
with the more famous Walter Scott?
We will never find out.

Yet the people lying here, all trod the selfsame valley
as we now do. Their hopes and fears are past
though once as real to them as ours are to us now.

At some future time, will someone look at our gravestones
and have the same thoughts?
By then we will lie at the same level as those who died
two centuries ago.

Newark Tower

On the field of Bannockburn
When Scotland's fortunes made full turn,
When haughty Southern turned to flee
And leave our ancient country free,
James Douglas had, as his reward
For battles fought both long and hard,
The Ettrick Forest as his fief
With King Robert's strong belief
That Douglas swords in Douglas hands
Would ever serve the King's demands.

That hope was vain
For James the Second of that name
Was jealous of the Douglas' fame
And fearful of their powers.
The Douglas he slew with his own hand
Then dispossessed them of their land
And seized their towers.

Nowadays the stately tower
Is no more the lady's bower.
Nor is it yet the meeting place
Of warriors of the ancient race.
No Scott or Douglas pace the floor
Nor open wide the iron door;
No minstrel to expand his theme
Nor tell the tales he saw in dream
And many years have passed since blew
The bugle of the Bold Buccleuch.

The River Ettrick

Frae the fit o a knowe on the side o The Pen
A trickle o water springs oot an then
Getherin strength frae the neeghbouren burns
Sets off doon the valley in shimmerin turns.
                              Thus Ettrick was born.

The mist clears the hill and the sooth wund blaws soft
Owre the steep slopes on the land that was lost
Tae planted Spruce trees across the hills ranged,
While the Ettrick rins on, unchanging, unchanged.

Bye Potburn and Braidgair, until wi a sweep
Skails intae the gorge o Will o Phawhop's Leap
Then Ouer Kirkhope, Crook Cottage and Shorthope until
It is squeezed in the rocks aside Cossarshill.

Doon thru the haughs, it passes nearbye
The auld gray kirk where ma ancestors lie;
Close bye are James Hogg, likewise Tibbie Shiel
And latter-day fowk that Ah hae kent weil
                        lie there in peace.

The river, now murmurs past cottage and haa,
Meanders thru haughs and the green waving shaw.
A lonely ferm hoose, standen steadfast and gray
Is lulled bie its sang as it rolls on its way
Until, at the fit o the Ramseycleuch brae,
                          the Tima joins in.

The Ettrick Floodplain – Now

The Celtic hunters came and went,
The Reivers tae, on mischief bent
An Ettrick Forest, yince sublime,
Had vanished in the mist o time.
Then some Norway Spruce was planted
On places where it wasnae wanted.

There came The Borders Forest Trust
Wi some ideas that we must
Restore it back as a floodplain
So it could be itsel again – as Nature intended.
They combined wi Forest Enterprise,
Then, no tae gie a big surprise
Tae Ettrick fowk; for, as was their right,
They were consulted on the site
          – and maist agreed.

Ten years o work, and thocht, and care
Transformed a plain yince soor and bare.
Now warmen sun brings honey smell
Frae willow herb or heather bell;
Wi gress and flouers the haughs are bloomen
The very air we breathe perfumen.

Then stop and listen if ye please
Tae hear the hum o worken bees
There is sae much that Ah could tell
But come and see it for yersel.

Frae Floodplain Tae The Kirkhope Linns

The Ettrick flows til at a turn
It joins up wi the Rankleburn
Past Tushielaw, close bye the Inn,
                    the Ettrick rins.

Ever moven and seldom at rest
On past Delorran, (East and West),
Then Gilmie, The Inch; another mile brings
Hyndhope, the ancient hunting seat o Kings
                    in Ettrick Forest.

Mair peacefae now; bye heugh and howe
Bye rashie haugh or gressy knowe
At Ettrick Shaws, the river bends
Tae cut thru rocks abin Brigend
                    at Kirkhope Linns.

Deep, deep doon, the river finds
Its wey oot thru the rocky Linns.
In wunter spate, a torrent rushen
Brawls owre the rocks, heavin, pushen
                    in wild cascade.

In summer time, sae soft its sweep
It soothes the troubled mind tae sleep
Beneath the shade o noble oaks
Where rowan trees cling tae the rocks
Or where a grove o fragrant pine
Is mingled wi the gracefae line
                    o silver birch.

Brigend Tae The Tweed

At Brigend, sae neat and trig,
The Ettrick rins ablow the brig
Adorned wi Harden's coat o airms,
Then Howford, Fauldshope and Bluecairn.
Aikwood Touer, on the southern side
Where Lord and Lady Steele now bide.

Here and there in Ettrick's stream
Are deep clear pools where salmon gleam;
Sae still the water there within
Stirred only bie a lazy fin.

It skirts the wuds aboot Bowhill
Past Cairterhaugh and Oakwood Mill
Tae join the Yarrae as intended
At Philiphaugh, they met and blended.

A savage battle here was fought
Twixt Highland horde and Lowland Scot
And here the Royal Cause was lost
When Leslie beat the Highland host
And slaughtered captives oot o hand
By Parliamentary Command.

Now at Philiphaugh ye'll see
Troot and salmon on TV
This concept brings us up tae date
Thenks tae Philiphaugh Estate
But now the conjoined rivers need
Resume their journey tae the Tweed.

F. CANNON

River   Tweed: Peebles – Coldstream
Words   Katrina Porteous
Images   Susheila Jamieson

Tittle-tattle Eddlestone, muttering of mill-lades,
Leithen, in harness, chattering of jeannies –
Sluicing down men and women from the hills:

Haad your wheesht, says Tweed
Softly to the Cuddy, the Weaver;
To the dried-up river-beds of labour;
To the stopped mouths of water.

                    * * *

Under Lee Penn, beside the whispering
Forests of Traquair, the shivering
Reflections of the flashlight dance and spin.
The salmon sniff the rain upstream. Joe sniffs the salmon;

And using the currents as the salmon use them,
He lets his cairn net curl, caa' back, until,
Drop by gleaming steely drop, the river
Gives up its secrets to him. Then he's off

Over the fence. The dark will swallow him
Like water. *Howden. Cowford. Leithen Pool.*
The Dam. The Cauld. A salmon leaps. Another.
The fish belong to no one but the river

'Got a romantic idea about poachers?
Don't you believe it. I've been a bailiff
Twenty year, and my father before me.

It's quietened off now. There's not the numbers:
Farmed salmon's finished the market.
I wouldn't go out till night time normally.

When I see a light, that's me on the mobile.
You don't know what they're carrying nowadays.
Slashing your tyres, smashing your vehicle –

Take it from me, they're only criminals.'

'I've cleeked them, I've netted them,
I've sneggled and I've guddled them;
I've gumped them in the eel-beds.
We were fin, fur and feather bairns',

Says Joe.
        'Tweed kept us.

Wi' cairn net, wi' bag net,
Wi' set net an' pullin' net,
It fed us. It claed us.
Put shoon on oor feet.'

And who's to argue?

Not Tweed,
Mingling its strange upwellings,
Its undertows, its cold currents,

Singing over the gravel,
Under the willow,
Over the cauld,

To ragwort-yellow Caberston,
To Scrogbank, to Rampy Pool,
To Rough Haugh and the Bogle,

You can make laws
Or break laws
But you'll quickly be forgotten:

The fish belong to no one
But the water
And tomorrow.

Stalactites hang
From the arches of Ashiesteil.
At Caddonfoot, at Fairnilee,
At the narrow bridge of Yair,

One by one, the ash trees
Trail their green fingers,
Sending thrills of silver
Through the river's silk,

Shoals of gold that flicker
Over the birch-bark,
Into the quiet forest,
Into the farthest shadows –

Tall reeds. Willows.
A basket, an arrow,
A deer slot, an echo,
Boats of skin and bark:

I was their road.
I kept them. Their shelter,
The forest. Every stalk
Glints like a weapon.

Shadows of trees, their bulk
Broken in the water:
The river gives them back,
Ghosts of their solid selves.

Got my Jock Scott, got my Silver Doctor,
Got my Black Ali Shrimp and my Garry Dog,
Got my Meg with the Muckle Mooth and Hairy Mary,
Got my Logie, my Jeannie, my Temple Dog;

Bring me a black-tipped fillet from a hare's ear,
A harl* from a feather in a partridge tail,
A tippet from a pheasant and a gamecock's hackle,
A stoat-hair, squirrel-tuft, red bull poll:
Come, wild spirit –
Catch me a salmon,
Spirit of the earth and sky and hill.

Got my yellow Ali Shrimp, got my Kinmont Willie,
Got my Meg in her Braws and my Dusty Miller,
Got my Cascade Shrimp, got my Stoat and my Comet,
Got my Junction Shrimp. Got my Monroe Killer.

In a land of spells, enchantments; whispers
Out of Wedale, out of Lauderdale, stories

Borne down the river like seeds,
Snagged in the heather,
On the whin's thorns;
Asleep under the Eildons:

Three witches. Three naked sisters.
Three sails on a black schooner.
Three teeth on the sky's jawbone:

Three sets of eyes that fix Tweed in one glare.

Towering, gnarled, volcanic, over the valley floor
That heaves, a sea, around them, they hold it spellbound;

And fold on fold, for miles, far fells and moors –
The bare, broad Cheviots, Ettricks, Lammermuirs –

Secret, wind-torn, disputatious grounds –
Are tense with expectation, or with fear.

Cursing the eye that looks into the future,
Winding back time to where it came from,
Three sisters. Three witches.

Three teeth on the sky's jawbone.

Under their shadow, Tweed is slowing, growing older.
Deeper, richer, more abundantly, it blooms,

Green tiers of birch, oak, alder, arching over
Banks of purple loosestrife, balsam and bees,

Reeds, silvery with warblers, and speckled thrushes
Rooting under the sycamores; and never more lovely

Than in the secret woods of Bemersyde,
Rinsed with its thousand birdsongs, dappled with gold,

Around the hushed stones of an older Melrose,
It loops; coils back on itself. Looks over its shoulder.

Prayers in the vaults;
Catechisms in the tracery;
Psalms in the buttresses:

And in the water, arguments.

Conversions. Baptisms. Blessings.
Writhing inside them,
Dark, ancient upwellings.

In an instant, Tweed is an adder.
Red veins dilate in it, anger
Flaring under its leaf-fringe. It is a colt.

As if its hair stood on end,
As if its nerves quickened, its skin trembles;
It breaks into white crests – leaps, churns, tumbles;

It is iron on the anvil,
Spitting cold sparks –
Oystercatchers' shrill shrieks.

It is a lion. The corkscrew torrent
Twists: gnaws
The red shank of rock.

A second later, it stretches, softens; relaxes.
It is a lamb. A shepherd. Its crook
Shelters a flood-plain of buttercups.

Berry Bush. Monksford. Cradle Rock. The Corbies.
Brockies Hole. Kipper Haugh. The Pot. The Webbs. The Bleedies.

It glides under Mertoun bridge, a green lullaby
Singing itself to sleep by Makerstoun,
Dreaming the streams, the pools, the bright miles before it.

The Duke's daughter has caught her first fish!
Isabella has captured a grilse.
It shines, a new moon, trapped in polythene –
Laughing, she runs with it across the lawn

Towards the sunlit turrets. She has brought it
From the smooth surface of the river, where the wind scribbles,
From the dark tunnel of trees, through open meadow
Beside the yellowing mound of Roxburgh Castle.

Great space, great sky surrounds her. Upon so little
So much depends. The river sighs. A fish
Leaps. The widening circles of its ripples
Catch the whole web of Roxburghshire in a mesh of light.

Somewhere far away a man is writing
Numbers in a ledger. The words 'Income Stream',
Jobs, projections, graphs and calculations
Flicker before him on a computer screen.

He wants to say they are the same: great families, salmon rivers –
Feeding the valley, keeping it green. But Isabella
Bursts from the sunshine through the dark doors, beaming.
She will show her shining burden to her father.

       * * *

What is making its way downriver,
Bobbing, turning?

A branch. A bucket. A bottle.
Nothing of value.

What is racing through Junction Pool,
Under the bridges,
Past the drowned islands,

Pulling its thread by Milk Pot,
Butterwash, elbowing onwards

Through bean and barley fields,
Through banks of crimson balsam?

It is life:
A bottle. A branch. A bucket.

It is time.
It is nothing of value.

The hymn carries far from Flodden
Over the rigs of cut hay,

Over the yellow rape, the stubble, the hissing wheat field
And the bent hawthorn tree;

Over the rich, sweet black and silver midden-heap.
So green,

So still, so drowsy: nothing stirs
Except the wren,

Singing, full-throated,
Fierce, belligerent,

As if it would join in.

      * * *

At Birgham a spider has drawn a map of the world,
Itself at the azimuth. All its meridians,

Stretching from clusters of purple campion,
Glint, as the breeze

Sends shivers of light through the ripening barley;
And over the broad, slow water that whispers: *Be still*,

All summer long, a small explosion of swallows
Angles and weaves.

Fifty miles away, the sky is clouding:
Rain darkens Tweedshaws. At Sprouston, the fish taste it.

A thousand miles away, the iron needle
Twitches for Carham in the salmon's icy blood.

Three thousand miles away, a spindle is turning.
Slowly, the barley eddies towards autumn.

The eels quiver. The spider thrums. The swallows
Gather the threads of the river, the skeins of the world.

River	Gala Water
Words	Tom Murray
Images	Rob Hain

Gala Water: rises in the Moorfoot Hills south of Gorebridge. It is 21 miles long and flows southwards through Stow and Galashiels and joins the River Tweed 2 miles west of Melrose

The wind whispers against my cheek.

I say to the wind.

I am me.

I am part of the largest family in this place called Earth.
I, and my brothers, sisters, cousins, flow, seep, leak,
gush, rush through just about everything and everyone.
I can cut through anything better, though slower, than
the sharpest knife.
I shape, define, gather people to me like a magnet.

Without me nothing lives

Without me gathering, storing, delivering memories
and feelings like an ancient priest from a religion
before time everything would be lost.
I have forever in every liquid particle of my being.

I say to the wind I need somewhere to gather breath..

MATALAN

While at the same time
I sit and chatter to Mother Tweed.
'Sometimes too many things happening.' I tell her.
'Did I ever tell you I was the first to know, apart from
the rain of course, that Sir Walter Scott was the author
of the Waverley Novels?'
'You've told me... Is that gunfire?'
'Only the cars rattling over Tweed Bridge.'
'And that?'

'Horses riding through me further down'

'Doesn't it hurt?'
'You get used to it'
'Many horses come this way!!'
'Common Riding O...'
'What?'
'Somebody's fallen off. What were you saying?'
'I'm finding it difficult being in so many places   at once'
'You think you've got a problem?'

MATALAN

And she was there and she wasn't. I knew the feeling.

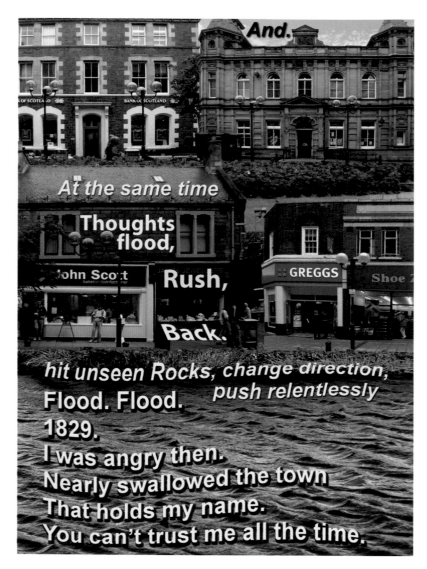

And.

At the same time

Thoughts flood,

Rush,

Back.

hit unseen Rocks, change direction,
push relentlessly
Flood. Flood.
1829.
I was angry then.
Nearly swallowed the town
That holds my name.
You can't trust me all the time.

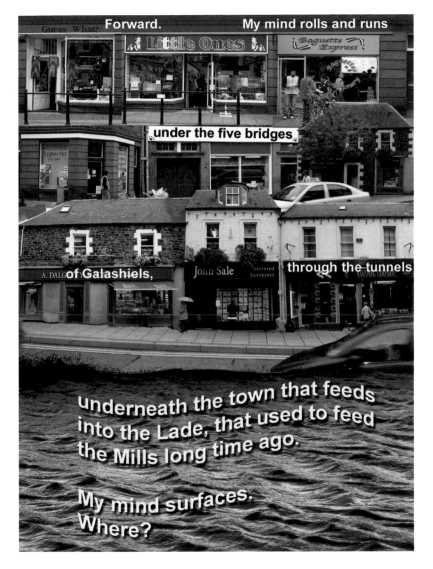

Forward. My mind rolls and runs

under the five bridges

of Galashiels, through the tunnels

underneath the town that feeds
into the Lade, that used to feed
the Mills long time ago.

My mind surfaces.
Where?

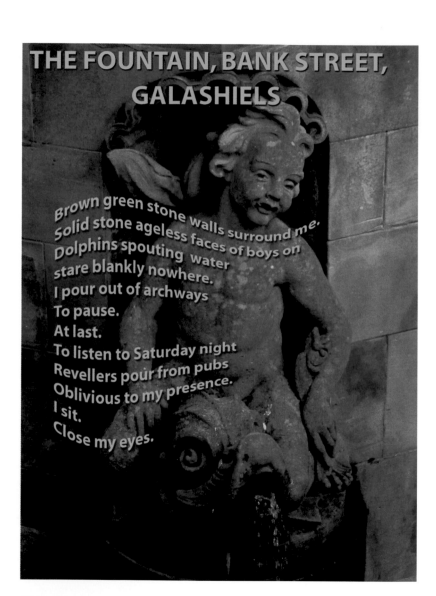

THE FOUNTAIN, BANK STREET, GALASHIELS

Brown green stone walls surround me.
Solid stone ageless faces of boys on
Dolphins spouting water
stare blankly nowhere.
I pour out of archways
To pause.
At last.
To listen to Saturday night
Revellers pour from pubs
Oblivious to my presence.
I sit.
Close my eyes.

I open them.
Something in the air.
I can smell it.
Rain hitching a lift with the wind.
'Looking over the bridge at the place they call B&Q' He says.
And we're there fast flowing against the sodden
grass verge and didn't the lingering smell of a
skinworks not dominate this area once upon my time.

How many times have I looked up from here and
everywhere else and seen them.
The same faces through the ages staring down at me
as if they know without knowing that the power
that drove the mills drives them.
This time a boy or nearly man stares down at me.
        Braw, braw lads o' Gala Water,
        Bonny lads o' Gala Water,
I listen to the flow of his thoughts.
I'm part of him as he's part of me.
He doesn't think that way of course.
I'm taken for granted I know.
I don't mind.
Maybe its better that way.
But 70% of him and everyone is Me.

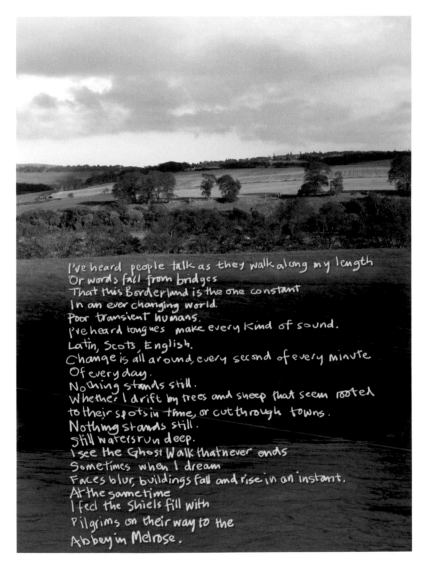

I've heard people talk as they walk along my length
Or words fall from bridges
That this Borderland is the one constant
In an ever changing world.
Poor transient humans.
I've heard tongues make every kind of sound.
Latin, Scots, English.
Change is all around, every second of every minute
Of every day.
Nothing stands still.
Whether I drift by trees and sheep that seem rooted
to their spots in time, or cut through towns.
Nothing stands still.
Still waters run deep.
I see the Ghost Walk that never ends
Sometimes when I dream
Faces blur, buildings fall and rise in an instant.
At the same time
I feel the Shiels fill with
Pilgrims on their way to the
Abbey in Melrose.

At the same time
I feel every mill along the Lade
from Lees to Abbots.
As one name is placed
On top of another.
Layer after layer
But the original is never
Quite erased. It's there
If you look.
It's there carried by
The wind and the rain
Dropped into my consciousness.
It's there if you stop awhile
Crossing that bridge,

Or lying in wait
For unsuspecting salmon.
And look deep into
My depths.
I'll be here,
Always.
Even if you think I'm asleep
I'll be listening, gathering.
It's what I do,

But not right now.
For I've managed to
get rid of the wind
and the rain and...

Time to pause,

Moon mirrored on my skin.
At times like this I feel curiously old
But always young.

My mind like a tap
Turned to off
But thoughts still there
Waiting.

I sink into my deep and shallow
Bed, dream what has gone before
Of the future waiting there
Somewhere.

Gala Water: rises again in the
Moorfoot Hills south of Gore

I am me.

River   **Leader Water**
Words   **Alice Mitchell**
Images   **Judith Rowan**

'The first water is Leider,
which runs mostly north to
south, hath its rise from
several heads. First from
Longmoormoss a burn
descends by Threeburnford
and Hartside, a third from
Seeinghill Cross by Greengelt,
and a fourth from Kolphupe by
Carfrae, with several others
which augment Leider, as
upon the north side Whelplaw
Water, Egerhope Water,
Bowndrich, Lidgertwood
Water, and Earlstoun Water,
upon the other side of Lauder
Burn.'

Sibbald's MSS, from A. Thomson, *Lauder and Lauderdale*

The Bondager

Consider Rivers.
They are always en route to
Their own nothingness. From the first moment
They are going home.

Eavan Boland

The Rising from darkearth,
headwater at Longmoormoss,
source, starting-place, womb,
moss and lichen etched in dawnlight,
wind gusts over the old commonty.
Once I filled my hand with mist.
The Dass is guardian of this hidden spot
out of sight of the grey-blue sea, seawater, rainwater,
earthwater rises, iris's bloom, earthwater rises, rises.

Ah wis born at Oxton Berwickshire. The 2nd o' March 1910 ... Oh, ma father he
wis always a ploughman. Well he wis the first ploughman. Well he gave the orders
ee ken ... and then he came to Booerhoose – the Bowerhouse. He wis working there
when ah wis born.

Ma mother used tae work on the farm afore she wis married. She wis a
bondager. She belonged Oxton in Berwickshire, oh she wis really Oxton ...

When ah wis four ah went tae Threeburnford. That wis aboot two miles
frae the Booerhoose ...

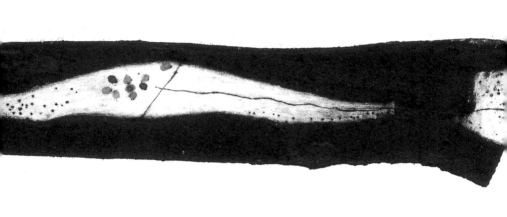

*Ah went tae Oxton School. Ah walked over the hill ... Ah went always the
hill, always the hill. Ah wis jist masel ... Ma mother yist to be feared ...
Ah wis never feared, no' even in the winter dark.*

Edith Hope

Letter to Edith

Dear Edith,
Bid 'ca canny' for
a boat of prints and poems,
Edith Hope, you are the source,
you really are the source,
liberties of image spring like wild flowers:
blue speedwell, wild thyme, tormentil,
orchids, red campion, a meadowfull still
on your Dass, your ledge of origin.

This bog is sweet, lifewater and rock,
wetland, willow-ed in greencopper,
a fastness with a skylark over.

Press grasses into footprints,
you wis jist yoursel, jist
the hill, always the hill,
*the ground, paper, pigments,
immense surface small.*
'Wee steps lassie,' mother calling.
water rises, a pool, liferise,
earth a bed for a splash of rain.

Threeburnford increases you
Edith, bairn, burn, muse,
pick a reed, make a tool,
you can be a spacemaker,
spill light and colour
where trout and salmon run.

Pinkblots, goudspinks –
Copper sulphate crystals
mixed with salt.
Wagtail, wren, swallow,
sparrow hawk and all the finches
on aluminium, mild steel and zinc.

The Packman

In the hills
where clouds touch
the path and my feet
are one.

In the valley
see how the sky
imagines itself
as a path of water.

Packman: 1. a pedlar, a travelling merchant, esp. in soft goods. 2. a type of cloud formation so called because of its shape resembling a man with a pack on his back.

The distance smirrs him,
he is ghost-written –
records of journeys
overland from sea coast
to places on the lesser river
do not exist. He wears three colours of blue.

It is maintained by some that Leader is a corruption of Laidur, which means the lesser water often discoloured. By lesser water it is meant that it is less than the Tweed …

Silence is the only music,
water flows where he treads,
he is no troubadour, no name
is rightly known for him,
he kens the rough Herring Road
and the Royal Burgh of Lauder. He sells thread.

By Wiselawmill

A fence is staked in mid air,

Great Flood August 1948. The flood left a great amount of damage to river
banks for the whole length of the Leader.

the wire could be a washing line,
posts – thick lime socks or tights
unsure of the cerulean sky,
small-scale cliffs crumble
to a shoreless corner,
the sinuous riverspine curves
midstream, defines sheer water-power in miniature.

The packman decsends from Addinstone,
he has travelled on foot from Haddington,
glad as ever, to see the Leader Water
in its wide haugh after Lammermuir's heights,
he crosses Wiselawmill footbridge.

Sharp oyster catchers
guard speckled eggs,
a nest of smallest pebbles
amongst whitened stones,
a dry eddy, an Andy Goldsworthy!

Iris * yellow * flags
Heron * gunmetal * surprised
Fort * pre-historic * horizon
Dabshead * stone * standing
Packman * knowe * then

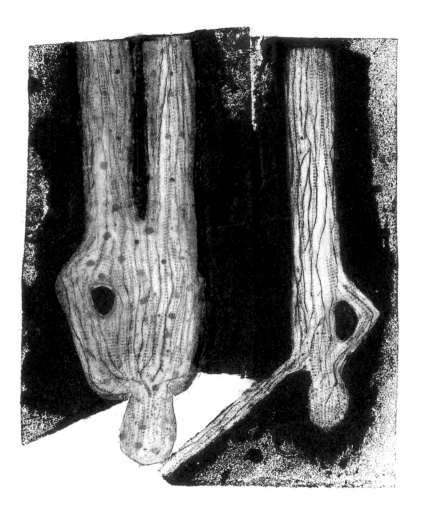

For Those Who Drowned

Your bones can stand and clothe
themselves in flesh as once they stood,
look how the woods refreshed seem new for old,
reflections in our river, time re-wound.

Upside-down your hearts can pound,
blood unburst and steady in your veins,
choked throats unfill and words come out aloud,
and would you curse to have your life again
or dance for joy? It really doesn't matter,
the river will not notice one way or the other.

Your bones can stand and clothe
themselves in flesh as once they stood
and hard toil and cold air, oh
cruel tongues and meagre fare
as well and warmth about the hearth
and love as once it was.

Love as once it was, will wrack
your mind then dry your wits
and if your time was not so long ago,
just *listen up* – the words we use can spill
a life, be mindful how the river flows
and how you go. *Oh! Oh!*
your bones, your bones, your bones, your red,
red blood, your bones.

& The Printmaker

Redpath River Path

Rain slants her enticing gossip,
summer slurred then cleared,
down below the Black Hill
showers manifest as Morse code,
Redpath river path shivers and swirls
on her bed of *Old Red Sandstone,*
swallows whole, plump pearls
released from a filigree canopy.

Listen! the skin of the water
tells and foretells –
like the Rhymer of Ercildoun,
its long imbued tale,
who are the fishers, millworkers,
covenanters, reivers spilling red and blue?

His pack and his step are lighter,
this red path goes beyond his area;
he rejoins the drover's road at Sorrowlessfield
(someone's son did not die at Flodden)
and might turn back at Packman's Burn.

Steps led us here, the steps are the rock
hidden in ancient river terrace,
like a sudden ascent in certain stories,
we must choose to circle the knoll
or forge into rusty forest,
find the bridge from past to present.

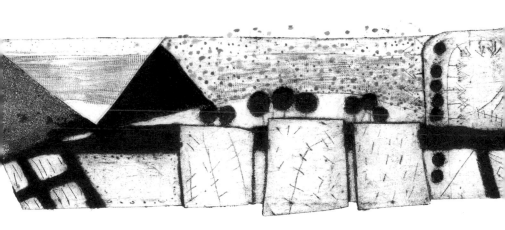

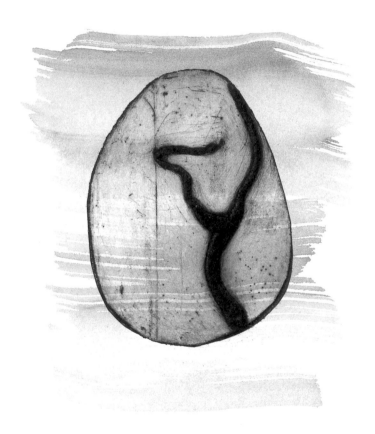

A Slice of Clear Blue Time

Hail Roman conquerors,
your old confabulations reverberate
at Trimontium on Tweed and Leader's confluence,
celebrate discoloured 'lesser' water's rose tones,
build a bridge or three, pillars of a community.

Forget not Longmoormoss,
Windygowle and Seeinghill Cross.

the very 'stanes' remade, shape-shifted
for a different journey towards the seagarden.

> *I never sleep, I dream*
> *renew, renew the blood*
> *in my ample arteries*
> *and the beat, time's moon-pulse,*
> *is icy or burning with daylight.*

A blue van stops on the A68,
we turn upstream,
sugarlift aquatint.

River	River Teviot
Words	John Murray
Images	John McGregor

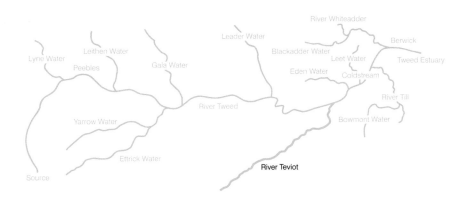

...The Bridge

The Cottage

Kay Braes

The Bend

Nicholson's Rock

The Castle

Garden wall

Slewans

Foghouse Nick

Chisholms

Segg Pool

Oak Strip

Maisondieu

Pothole

Annie End

Canty's cast

Try me Well

The Long Pool

The Wash Pool

Mill Pool

Gogaren

The Haughs

The Viaduct

Bloody Breeks

Quarry Pool

Sunlaws Mill

Turn Pool

Ninewells

Sandbed

Rock Cast...

Somewhere,
water of another millenium
can emerge

from the join
between clay and sand
basalt and mudstone

What age am I?
molecular lobby of all
that's been or will be,

from the join
between granite and lime
shale and slate.

What age the sum?
of guests and inmates
both long and short term,

Somewhere,
water of another age
can emerge,

the soul
the senses
but a pickle electricity.

as the seepage of millennia
in transit between
sink and issue, issue and sink.

Time seeping from the join
between the porous
and the impervious.

What age at Ninewells?
What age the Tinkler Burn?
What age the Foghoose Stream?

Time seeping between
the porosity of the past
and the opacity of the future.

At Ninewells
I am the ninth part of nothing
and the nth part of everything.

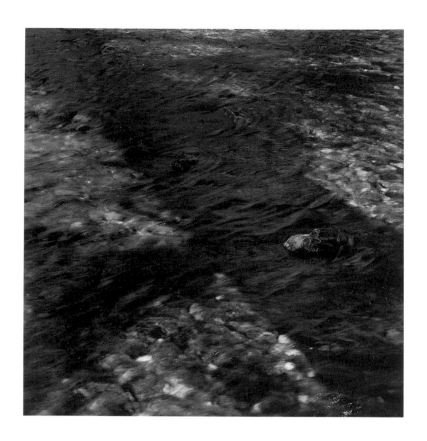

I lie supine
below the watershed.

My skeleton
defines the catchment.

I stretch my limbs
like an unfurling frond.

I dig my heels in.
My fingertips claw the sand.

My hips mould
mute substance,

which I've both
made and undone.

The soles
of my feet are stained with peat

There's grit
beneath my fingernails

Fluid courses
through my open limbs,

collects and
conjoins in my torso,

outflows in the
final confluence of memory,

laps between boney shores
of mind and mindlessness.

The cycle closes complete,
and as empty as a contour.

Issue and sink are both
contained and confused in me.

I false cast,
cast and cast again.
I shoot a long

and slender line of latency
over the soft surface
of darkly moving pools.

An untestable
hypothesis unrolls.
A lifestory writ upon water.

I mend the curve of my line
continually and upstream
as she comes round with the current.

My fly fishes at the proper depth.
I take stock, adjust and amend.
At the dangle, I delay.

The fly hangs by a thread.
It is deadly at the take –
a dagger of Damocles.

The latent image of a thought fish
forms in the camera of my mind,
the emulsion of my memory.

The aperture of my purpose
closes on its focus.
He fished meaning from the unseen.

In memory of Ted Hughes

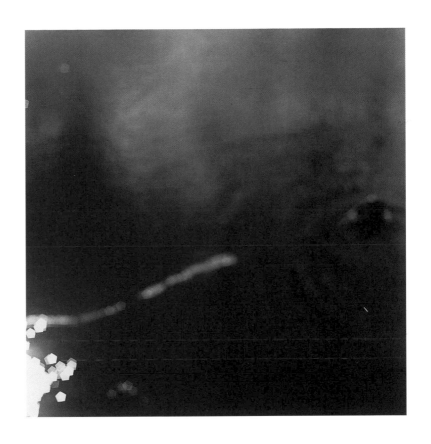

I peer into
crystal pools.

I cannot
see surface.

I cannot
determine depth.

My stick
touches the riverbed.

I look
into your eyes.

I cannot
guess your depth.

I drown
in the dark of your pupil.

Distant lights from the back of your eye
dazzle my vision.

I have no means
of taking your measure.

Fause man lay on Tivie side,
an a whitret he spied wi his ee.
Question mairk lowpin atween salmon pools guid,
Canty's, the Well an Maisondieu.

Kelt fish deid on Tivie side
nae een an a kype that cannae steik
washed up an left bi winter's flood,
tailed aboot a dried bit cleik.

Fause man slept on Tivie side,
an a whitret pyked oot baith his een,
smooled inby his lug
an sooked his brainpan clean.

O pick me up ma smooth white skull
wi yer haun sae quaiched an warm.
Uplift me slow an ask of me
did ye win the redd an did ye spawn?

Did ye win tae yer hindmaist destinie,
yer true tributrie?
Did ye win tae yer ain mairch dyke?
braid seas encompassed in a syke.

I lay my palm upon the land.
My fingers stretch over the relief.

I cover the catchment
within my watershed.

Veins on the back of my hand
are tributaries and confluences

leading from
issue to sink, sink to issue

from springs at my fingertips,
to seas at the heart of me.

Rain washes from
my waterproof skin.

I cannot hold the world
within my grasp,

I cannot keep a drop of water
upon the back of my hand.

I am the water boatman
twin oarstrokes, fleeting
footfalls on the fluvium.
Snail shine behind.

I skiff the
the surface tension of moment.
I occupy the meniscus
between past morass and future vapour.

I'm buoyed by the ocean,
suspended by the sky,
plying perpetually between shores
both fancied and forgotten,

between here and there
between now and then.
I'm both compass
and lighthouse,

I'm a pronoun,
indicative of nothing
but the demonstration
of abstraction.

I'm both ferryman
and passenger, pilot
and piermaster, harbour
and hazard, anchor and abyss.

River	Eden Water
Words	Robert Quilietti
Images	John Behm

Eden Water

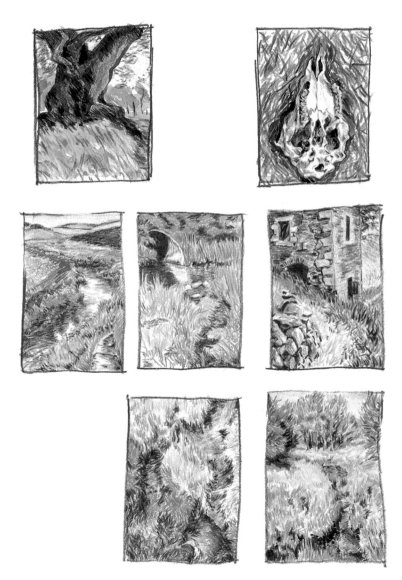

Walking The Edge Of Eden

Prologue, *prÔ'log*, n. an introduction to a poem, play, etc.

DAY 0: Sitting in front of a Bondi Blue Macintosh computer.

It's all about expectations, isn't it … know what I mean? Write about a river, write me an aquatic novel, spin us a sailor's yarn, cobble together a watery poem that scans but doesn't rhyme, and what are you doing? – Setting up expectations.

'Oh, it's about a river, that'll be depressing – pockets full of stones and a dreary last paddle. Like the curtain call of that miserable old trout – Virginia Wotsername.'
I can almost see the newts and tadpoles dodging the writer's feet, bubbling voices whispering *'dead man walking'*. But that's what you expect. Tragedy, misery. Worse still … poetry. It's what you expect, maybe what you want. What you think you need.

But you're wrong. (It's only part of the story.)

DAY 1: Begins at Corsbie Tower, close to source of Eden Water.
Eden, *ê'dn*, n. the garden of Adam and Eve; a paradise.

You can start walking the Eden at either end – the source or the confluence – *it makes no difference.* Start in the middle if you want – say, Stichill Linn (a cascading Easter Egg for Eden's virgins), or try dodging the fletcher's arrows to stroll (unticketed, so look to your own conscience please) onto the rolling lawns of Mellerstain's lakeside. It makes no difference. You see, it's all temporary, surface without substance. Rivers? – Illusions, that's what they are. Each and every one. Illusions. Listen to me. I should know. Illusion has been part of my life. Check out my credentials. Made a good living from illusion (before the illness dropped by to say *'hello laddie'*). I should know … so … listen to me and think about it.

Wherever you're standing, riverbank or bridge, giving the trickling waters the big Pooh Sticks stare, you'll never be seeing more than an instant of the river's life. Only an instant. Shorter than an anxious heartbeat. Try looking at a rippling on the surface. Point it out to a friend. Where is it now? … *'Over there! Look! Aw! Too late!*

It's gone.' Buddy boy's right ... *it was there but now it's gone.* Moving towards the mother flow: The Tweed like Hank Williams, like Tom Joad – 'Movin' On' – leaving nothing behind, expecting nothing ahead.

No, don't get me wrong. I love the river. Magical, that's what it is, that's what they all are. Magical. Like I said before – I should know. Remember that tiny island of rocks and grasses we passed a while back? Just by Gordon Mill, down from the wobbly stepping stones. Four boulders bisecting the waters. Tall grasses struggling for space in between the stones. Lichen and moss patches in overlapping shades of green. It's just that, rocks and plants, but it's perfect. Put in the only place it could be put. Perfect. A cosmic feat of sleight of hand. Sliding the pea under the least likely walnut shell, at just the right moment. Rocks. Plants. Water.

Try taking that memory along to your garden centre: *'Here you go, pal, build that at the bottom of my garden, please'.* Know what you'd get? A water feature; pipes and cables, humming pumps and pink gravel. And the knowledge that it can't be done, that you can't replicate the magic that dots the river. That it's not ours to take.

An alder leaf drops to the water's surface where it twitches and trembles like the hands of the stranger I sat beside at yesterday's support group. Neil/Nyall/Lyall ... something like that. Linen suit, crumpled just right, and tan brogues that had been force fed Dubbin since birth; shoes that sang out *'hand made'*. A dapper man but with a tremor that rattled his upper torso from scalp to fingertips. A crippling twitch, mechanical in regularity, seismic in intensity.

'Been diagnosed long?' It's the classic opener, the Parkinsonian icebreaker, the equivalent of 'Are you dancing?' He answered in a voice so thin that I couldn't catch his reply, couldn't put a timeline to his symptoms. Couldn't calculate how long I had before ... well ... you know what I mean. His coffee slopped about in a child's cup, twin handles, plastic, with a striped straw jutting from the spout. Red and white swirl. A tiny barber's pole signifying not haircuts or highlights but rather, Sickness and Disease.

Chronic. Degenerative. Incurable. Sodding well incurable.

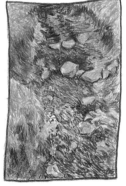

DAY 2: West End of Hume Village; on the North Bank of River Eden.
Myxomato'sis, n. contagious viral disease of rabbits. [Gr. Mx, mucus.]

My neglected boots (Timberlands, blood red) let water ooze from the peat bog through the pores of the dying leather. I wonder if Neil/Nyall/Lyall (Dapper Man with the Shaky Hand) would be offended by my sub-standard footwear care regime. My socks are wet. My toes wrinkled, raisined by Eden's Waters. My forehead wrinkles too. Seems stuck like that these days. Wrinkled. Corrugated. Creased with rage. Forehead furrowed by the diagnosis, belly churning at The Prof's nonchalance.

'... *other people told you ... friends, family ... you saw it yourself. You knew you were slowing down, almost freezing over. Stagnating. Well, now you know why. Not much you can do about it. Not much. Not really.* [He decides that saying 'pretty hefty' in a singsong voice would add a lightness to his words.] *I'm going to prescribe some prêt'ty hêf'ty medication*'. He scribbles the two words in the margin of MY case notes, underlining the stress points, not wanting the ad-lib to drift away, forgotten like yesterday's river current. Sure, the pills work, they go some way towards making me look normal, softening my face-mask, loosening my shoulders. But there's always that fraction that isn't used, that accumulates at the raggedy edges of my brain until, wallop!!!, I'm left nauseous by confusion, angered by weakness.

The start of the walk had been tough today. An excess of fences crossed my path, all armed with barbed wire. The Devil's Rope – they've got a museum full of the stuff somewhere in America.

Y'all git yourself over to the Scottish Borders, country cuzzins, it's everywhere over here. All the fences need climbing though, if I want to track the River Eden to its meeting with the big one, to see it swallowed whole by the Tweed. And barbed wire needs careful clambering. Each attempt leaves me weak. Trembling.

Neil/Nyall/Lyall.

Bespoke in the shoe department.

Drinking coffee through a straw.

Sad old sod.

My feet are wet, my feet are weary and the Eden drifts by, sparkling and chill. Why not? I pull the soggy footwear off and dangle my feet in the cool water. The memories are immediate and vivid: boyhood afternoons of truancy from Berwickshire High spent doing just this.

Walking the Edge of Eden. Alone. Cooling sweaty feet in the waters. Using curled toes to pick up pebbles from the riverbed. Trying to beat my own record. Quantity, not quality: that's what pebble picking needs. And today, I'm doing well. The morning pills are, at last, kicking in just fine. Putting the tremor on hold for today's share of The Prof's alleged seven years.

'Take the drugs and you might get Seven Years [he spoke the words in letters of filigree gold], around Seven Years [filigree gold and gift-wrapped for good measure] – if you can cope with the side effects.' Conditional. Good news, hope, improvement. Sit facing across a neurologist's desk and these things become conditional. I take the drugs, regular, like The Prof said. Even bought a little gadget that tells me when to take my pills.

'TIME TO TAKE YOUR PILLS!!!! TIME TO TAKE YOUR PILLS!!!!'

The voice is female; half Madison Avenue, half Microsoft, and if I ever meet her, I swear I'll strangle the irksome witch. But the Prof hadn't finished with me yet. 'You'll be an old man by then . . . zimmer, wheelchair – you'll probably be past caring. Seven Years of diminished symptoms: reduced tremors, touch more mobility – that kind of thing. Could be as much as Seven Years . . . provided that the side effects don't become too horrendous.' (Nice one, Prof . . . glad tidings of comfort and joy – and no mistake.)

But I must admit, today is a turning into a good day. Five or six toe-stones with every plunge. Haven't lost the technique. Not yet. Nope, still got my toe-curling abilities. I lean against the blackened trunk of a fallen bog oak, drying my feet on handfuls of fern leaves, scrubbing hard. My damp boots go back on, laces left untied. Takes me an age to tie laces or fasten buttons. Velcro? An admission of defeat, my friend. Don't wish that upon me just yet. No, no, no . . . you misunderstand. Defeat I can accept. Defeat I can do. It's Velcro that terrifies me.

A desperate and pained cry comes from the clump of purple borage behind me. I turn to see a rabbit crouching low to the ground, small enough to be only a few weeks old, small enough to be 'A Bunny'. The flesh covering its chest cavity pounds, tiny heart racing towards bursting point. Fear and exhaustion bulge his eyeballs from within. Adrenaline streamlines his ears flat back against his shoulders and sleekens his fur. I step closer, the rabbit doesn't budge. I reach forward, still no reaction. I grab the creature by the throat and hold it close to my face. Grey froth foams from his chattering lips and dribbles over my knuckles. The scrawny creature seems to be sliding from my grasp and I retch as I realise his pelt is peeling from the flesh beneath. I look into the creatures scarlet eyes and shudder. The red glow coming from within ripples and heaves. Pulsates. Rotting brain matter, infected by an alien disease, an introduced virus, dribbling from its nest in the rabbit's skull down, poisoning its body with infected tissue. Decay glowing red through dying eyes. I lob the beast into the water and watch it struggle for a moment before it drifts out of sight. Gone. Vanished. Maybe never really there.

DAY 3: Junction of River Eden and River Tweed, Edenmouth Bridge.
Confluence, *kon'floo-ens*, n. a flowing together, as of rivers.

The bridge fails to inspire me. Insignificant toy-town structure offering nothing in the way of grace or beauty. A utilitarian ford over the waters. But I do find the parapet to be a comfortable height for leaning against. No need for tippi-toes to get a view of the seamless joining of the two rivers below. Just a gentle stretch, pleasant, making me feel like the scrawny matchstick men on the physiotherapist's exercise sheet.

'Exercise twice a day, if you can find the time.' I study the firmness of his muscles. Shoulders pinned well back, arms swinging to accentuate his springing step. I walk along behind, shoulders sloping, arms stiff. Shuffling steps and a forward tilt of my body give the appearance of a badly trained monkey with a whiplash injury. 'Don't strain, gentle stretches – that's all you need. Should slow down the inevitable.' He doesn't turn to look at me when he speaks. Just keeps a steady pace, rubber soles of his trainers squeaking against the lino floor. And I do try to follow his regime but even the most gentle exercise adds to my constant weariness. Leaning over the bridge is as physical as I intend being today. I drift into the Pooh Sticks Stare: the reverie we all sink into watching a river's flow on a bright afternoon. The glassy-eyed alpha state that feels so good. My anxieties slip through my pores, floating down to the waters, to be buried at sea along with my rabbit. My mouth fills with the taste of copper as the hallucination begins.

There he goes . . . Neil/Nyall/Lyall . . . Master of the Uncontrolled Tremble, holder of the plastic cup of Premier Division Tremor . . . off on a trip in a leaky coracle, down the Tweed, spinning as his boat passes over my Eden Water's flow.

And the star shows itself to me. Sitting on the surface of a rock, close to the riverbank. A pentacle shimmering from the wake thrown up by Dapper Man's vessel. Five points of light showing highlights from a life too short, too little lived in to make room for a cuckoo disease. Not today, Mr. Parkinson. Take your twitches and your palsy off to another body, one ready to receive you. Today I'm off to claim my fallen star. I reach down to pick up this symbol of hope. A moment of confusion before I twig . . . it's a biscuit, it's a sodding, sodden cast-away biscuit that squelches through my fingers, dropping onto the water, drifting on the surface towards the meeting place.

And there the crumbs from my short-lived star twirl, spinning from one tiny whirlpool to the next. Marking the stretch where the two waters meet.

And the whorls and the crumbs dance a jig on the surface of the broth that is The Tweed. Reeling towards the horizon, diminishing, their journey towards insignificance revealing more than just the exact point of confluence.

River   Tweed: Coldstream – Berwick
Words   Katrina Porteous
Images   Susheila Jamieson

Deep, slow, oily, sinister,
Under the viaduct, by the tall poplars,

Hedged by an island of willow and alder,
Gravy-brown soil washes down from the Till,

Darkening Tweed – a stain, a shadow,
An English tune in a similar idiom;
Widdershins swirls of drumly water.

There are two sides to every border.

* * *

But what's this?
        Round the next twist,
                under the hogweed,

Just at the bow of the meadow, in sight of the cobweb
Curves of the Union Chain Bridge, under the trees,

Something is trying to claw its way up to the surface
From very deep.

Green swirls.
        Long fingers.
                Weed.
                        The musky scent of it.

The salt.

The sea.

'Ye read the winds. Ye watched the signs,
Ye'd wait for the Point when the tide come forward –
That was wor harvest, Point; an' mind,
They're away t' the river afore ye know it.

That's how they've survived all these generations.
Aah'm tellin' ye, nets never ruined the river.
Hundreds a' years a' the nettin' stations
An' salmon come back the same as ever.

Now it's off wi' the nets an' it's back to nature.
Whatever wor natural instinct to catch 'em,
A fish on the rod is worth more to the river.
These days it's money that keeps things natural.'

A flash. A gleam. The slap, kick, thump,
Smack on the shore is a shock: five salmon
Out of their element, furious, violent,

Beautiful as a birth. The shining
Muscle and guts of the river loosed
Around their feet, the four men stoop:

A tumult. Wing-beats. For an instant
The same wild current courses through them.

Croak from the reed-beds, Bob Morrison, Bob Morrison,
The rouk's on the water. It's time we were leavin',
From Pedwell to Sandstell. The border is shiftin' –
It's more for the rods and more for the river.

      * * *

Under the A1's arterial hurry
Old Tweed spreads out, broad and slow and easy,

Its surface feathered by the breeze. All blowsy,
It laps, sucks, toothless, at the undercut mud-bank,

A glacial boulder, a traffic cone, a stone-age fish-trap,
Slowly sinking into ooze and slime, or slowly uncovered.

High overhead, their wings up-lit at sunset,
Armies of herring gulls row their white ghosts downriver.

Over the flat haugh, over the salt-marsh, they muster
Out of two countries – over the wheat fields, the ramparts,

The sewage plant, the housing estates, the rotting dockyards,
And drift on Yarrow Slakes like snow – one flock.

At Whitesands and Abstell, Calot and Blakewell,
At Carr Rock, at Crow's Batt, at Gardo an' Hallowstell,
Haul in your gear, lads, it's time we were leavin'
From Canny and Pedwell to Farseas and Sandstell.

Ahead, the Royal Border Bridge. It is a gate
Sorting this side from that side. It combs the broad water.

Perched on the mud-bank, the haughty swans clap their wings:
Here's Berwick, perched on its high horse, looking down on England.

The tide is sucking out. Its swirls and eddies claw away

The knuckled roots of pines and fossil forests, collor and seeds,
The silts, soils, stones of prehistoric oceans, dragged from far upstream,

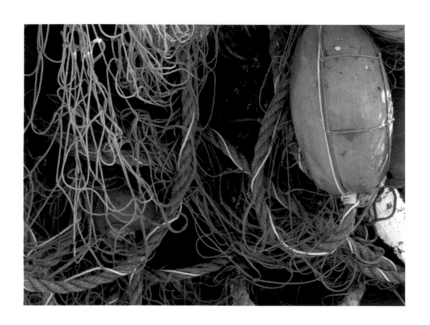

The spawn, the snails, the shrimps, the eels, the smolting salmon – millions strong,
Their populations scattering

To far-flung places of migration and desire, tumbled and whirled
And rolled together in the dark, the cold

Salt, shifting place where river ends and sea begins

To wind all journeys back to where they came from.

It's this that I was looking for,
Says Tweed:

Oblivion.

On Spittal beach, among the sticks and broken shells, strips torn
From desiccated black
Plastic bin-bags metamorphose into crackling scraps
Of bladder-wrack,

And tubes of polypropylene become the woomlick kex,
And strands of willow bough,
The hitches, bends and splices of a thousand long-discarded
Nylon tows;

As if, in this great glittering meeting, weaving, marrying, relaxing,
Tweed lets go
Its cumulative weight of contradictions; memories, imaginings – all borders
Flow

Into one another, and the line – the human, managed, measurable shore –
Is lost
To whirling currents; and, beyond, the spiral stream
Of stars and dust.

On the farthest spit of coarse brown grit,
Sandstell,
Wind shivers a few blades of lyme grass, and the sun picks out
A bleached sheep-skull,

And wound around it, rags and tatters that were once
A salmon net;
So tangled up, their fortunes river-ravelled and impossible
To separate.

River **Leet Water**
Words and Images **Nigel Bridges**

An almost trivial reference to the Leet Water, as

'a rivulet of the Merse'

in The Imperial Gazetteer of Scotland, 1854, may seem unflattering but the Leet is indeed little more than a ditch for much of its course. No amount of artistry can raise its lowly nature to status of mighty tributary, but that does not mean it lacks interest.

Were the attentive walker to pause along its banks they might observe the leaves of ash, elm, hawthorn, aspen, willow, or even feathers floating slowly downstream. Closer scrutiny might also reveal the leaves gently rotating to a preferred axis of alignment as they make their journeys.

Pick a leaf from the water and examine the network of veins on the back of the blade. The veins run in a neat pattern from the leaf tip to the stalk pointing towards the tree. Even the leaves arranged on the branches that overhang the Leet follow this directional bias.

Examination of any map showing physical properties reveals that river systems follow this same pattern as they carry surplus water from high ground to the sea.

LEET WATER

The Leet runs almost parallel with the Tweed for some 7 miles separated by approximately $3\frac{1}{2}$ miles. However, while the mighty Tweed is flowing north-east towards Berwick, the Leet is going in the opposite direction away from the sea. It can only be imagined what glacial mis-scrapings caused this strange sense of direction.

The Leet rises at Doons Law, 70m above sea level, among the golden wheat fields of Leetside. It has barely dropped 25 metres before it gains directional sense.

It turns, almost at right angles, between Grizelrig and Darnchester West Mains, and makes for the Tweed, which it joins at Coldstream, a point further west than its source. This peculiarity of the Leet results in frequent overflows.

Coldstream

RIVER TWEED

Mayfly *Ephemera danica*

life's time

may fly

one chance

to try

the dance

The life span of the adult mayfly lasts a few hours. In this brief time the mayflies mate in flight, after which the male dies. The female lays her eggs on the surface of the water before also dying.

Ephemeral dancer

—

time

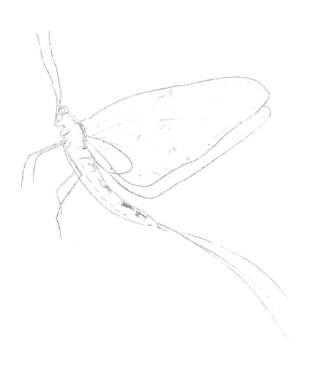

ILLEGAL
IMMIGRANTS

Three boxes from a series of ten: 2004: Giant Hogweed stem, sycamore, various other materials and finishes. Ranging from 215mm to 75mm high x 35mm diameter. Near the mouth of the Leet are large tracts of Giant Hogweed. Various attempts are being made to control this highly invasive plant. In my mind this raises interesting parallels with human migration.

ASYLUM
SEEKERS

NATURALISED
CITIZENS

TRUMPED

.

Centuries overlap in this view across the Leet Water from a pasture beneath Hatchednize. The ruined castle is framed by the diamond (an ace) of the pylon. The power lines run north and south across the border.

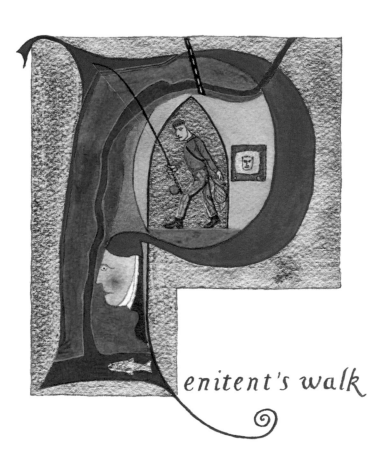

Penitent's walk

by the Leet's

cold stream

River River Till and Bowmont Water
Words Linda France
Images Birtley Aris

TWO RIVERS

'Water is good for all living things.
It flows without thinking where it is...

..... going'
Tao Te Ching: Lao Tsu

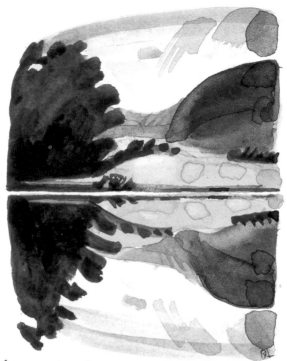

'Tweed said to the Till
what gars ye rin sae still?
Till said to Tweed
Though ye rin wi' speed
And I rin slow
Yet where ye droon yin man I droon twa'.

Traditional Verse

Bowmont Water

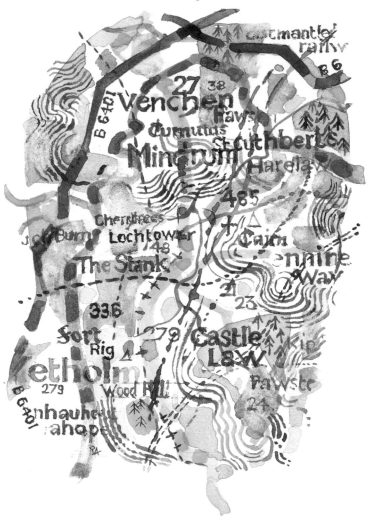

If there is a gateway,
there must also be a threshold,
a border to tread between two worlds.
There is in and out. There is open and closed.
You are a gypsy. You are not a gypsy.
Keep walking. Even if you don't know where
you are going, keep on walking.

You are climbing Venchen Hill, looking for
the Virtue Well. You want to make a wish.
You want its holy water to soothe your thirst.
The gorse is growing wild, the trees
have lost their way. Even the walls
are falling. You cannot find the well.
KEEP walking.

There is a lake. It drowns trees.
A grey ellipse, it is home for birds
that swim out of their element - moorhens,
gulls, a family of swans. This is valley,
where earth accepts the fact of water.
It cools you with its whisper of agate, jasper.
Keep on walking.

River Till

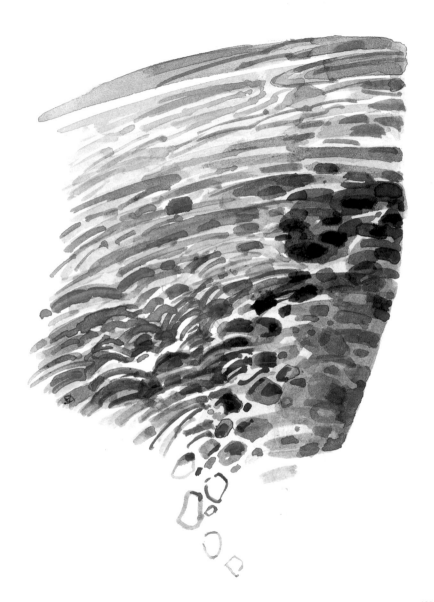

You thought the sign said 'To the *Brace*
of Both Nations,' where King James fell;
the book tells you '*Brave*.' You don't know
what made the scars in the side of Twizel Bridge,
what march, what battle; only read
the beauty of lichen, freedom of sycamore wings.
Keep on walking.

This is the place where two rivers meet,
the Till and the Tweed. It is a long Y,
a beginningless, endless question you'll ask
the Himalayan Balsam's purple mirror.
This side is England; the other Scotland.
Can't go forward, can't go back, can't stay still.
Keep walking.

Past the mill at Etal, there's a broken footbridge. Wooden steps rise into nowhere, can't cross the river. A blistered sign still warns no more than two people must walk it at once. The sound of the water spilling over the weir rinses your ears.
Keep on walking.

there is more pleasure in bridges than gateways.
Where one element joins another, it doesn't add up
to two. You count them on your fingers:
earth, water, air; today, yesterday, tomorrow;
Bowmont, Till, Tweed. Always more
than you think there is. Keep walking,
friend, there are three of us, and we are ocean.

TWIZEL *Twizel Bridge* Twizel Castle

Finger Burn

ST CUTHBERTS

Tweedmill

Twizel Mills Cherrytrees *Yetholm Law*

Kirk Yetholm TOWN YETHOLM *Yetholm Loch*

River **River Whiteadder and**
Blackadder Water
Words **Colin Donati**
Images **Pauline Burbidge**

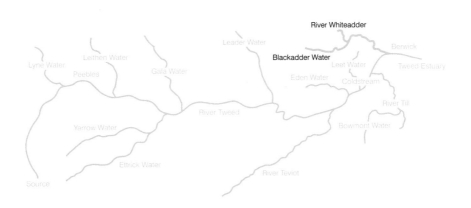

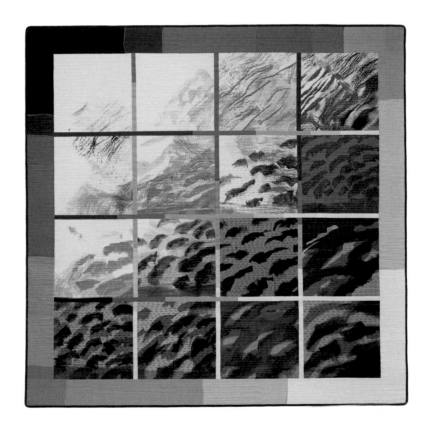

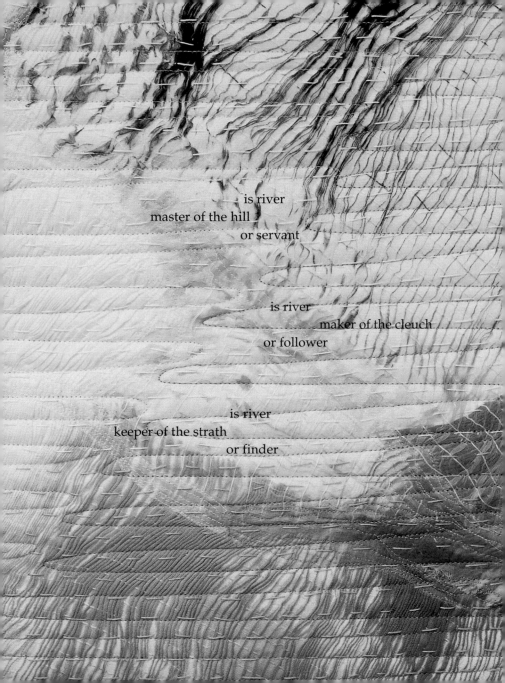

is river
master of the hill
or servant

is river
maker of the cleuch
or follower

is river
keeper of the strath
or finder

                    ev n
)s e e(
                    a t
  d r k
          i n th e   hi g h
                                   n gh t
      see k(
              bur ns
  o f cl nt   d od
)s ee   in th e L
  the r(s l w sy k e   fr m th e cairns
      the)r gu r l   s ee(p
    no on e lon e s   )rce
                    m (mer rmu   rs
              w h er e the wind)s an d
  and h rring r ds   w a te(rs   s h e a r
      r the laws the   peat   i   dd en glack(s
  where wind   wh)ere it   )se e
      here   and just one t urn   and
                  a n d   at p(sh iel
                  and su
)where none was before and(——
                            ddenly it's   *reservoir*
      where   almost immediately *loch* that
                  someone's put there in their sleep
          and high hill farm has a *shore* and   w
      monstrous entity   where glen   once
          la contrée de Landinore   below limnetic depths   of
  for a while at   least   *trespassa outre*   *sans arest*
      limnetic depths of   collects and   of water   of

a re se rv oi r a wai tin g th i ng
a r e s er vo ir a l i pp er t hin g
n o wat ers tr a ce d t o one lon e sourc e
n o l an guage trac ed to o ne s ole sou rce
n o st or y he l d to one o ne s o ur c e
n o h ist ory tra ced t o on e lon e caus e
e ndl es s r es tle s s of r i ve rs
al l hi s o ry mer ely   s and cha n ge
ly is and   and ch n ge is al l
a l l s to ry m rely is a n   nge
r l y is and   and   is l
n   a ll l angu ag e m   ly i s an   n e
no r ef e p   oints a   nd l t   i s al l
a ll r v er voi r nts m r l y are an d   l e
n   o refe r ent po i n ts d   l gh t i s all
no   r fer n t p oi nts n o fix d of l i t se lf
n o si ng le r efe   r ent p   o int   o l i g ht
t h e   m oon w r it i ng itsel f
o ver an d ov er ag ain an agai n
a   c h ine se c hara cte r on the lo ch
of d rk l gh t bli n d r estles s s urf ace
al l dee ps al l r es ervoi r s a ll de e p s
t he w orl d ov er an d overa o v er ag n
s imultlanelo us anld cotnst nt
al ml ind r all iv ers als le n tienc e a le vle nts
s o wffste ert li p per on tl e s urff a ce
a   ndn o observe r
an ye t a ye i t aa ll l li ls
aa arou n u s an ar oun m e
h il ls le riv er l la nlg ul a gl e sel n t ien ce e lvlen ts

Whitadder loops roun Cockburn Law
be Robber's Cleugh, be Greenhope Weil
be Hairie Craigs, be Scrogie Wood
be Shannobank and Butterwell
be Edin's Hall Broch and Strait Lowp
Elba, Hoardweel and Deil's Dungeon
Humbles Knowe and Stoneshiel Hill
where out she fa's to lower grund
and lowsed, gangs forrit on her roads
round Anger ma Heart, Baramill
Cumledge, Paradise and Marden
Kilnick, Edrom, Todheugh, Blue Braes
Hyndhaugh Brae and Haudgate Hole
bi Chapel Haugh, bi Gallaws Law
bi Steeple Heugh, bi Murder Den
bi Swallow Heugh, bi Harper's Heugh
wi Blackadder (twa floods nou joined)
by Patie's Cove, by Newton Braes
by Witches Cleuch, by Raven's Knowe
by Clarabad and Cawderstanes
syne wunnin parallel wi Tweed
slups tentless ouer a wordless border
and's out – by New Mills, Canty's Brig
…wha'll can recite this litany
and sense whit stories its names kythe
w ha'll can r ecite this litan y
a nd haud lang h ist ories aye intac t
w h a'll ca n r eci t e thi s lita n y
sou n s l eid s lang tin t gh aist terra ce s
d et ached nou f ae ts r i ver s c ou rs e . . .

Stood here my lane sel in September heat
On Twinlaw and there she is, the haill braid Strath
Raxed out below frae here to Cheviot,
A meikle runkled flair aneath the luft
Of flood-plain till that – man! fair taks the braith;
The hinmaist syndings of a moontain range
That yinst stood prood here, high as the Himalias
Does the-day, whaur Asia meets India.
Nae hill inveigles itsel mair intil
The Border consciousness nor Cheviot does;
Blue Cheviot, yon auld Devonian, skied
Aye lownlike on the suddron mairch of Merse;
Her saft faur line, yon blue kenspeckle bou,
The talisman that gaes til aw my days
Their deepest hert-felt referent-pynt.
Ye near can sense the curvature of earth here
Hyne frae this vantage pynt: to wast the Eildons,
Our meikle wheel hub; to east a glisk o sea
Skinklan in licht ayont the port of Berwick,
(Thon pairtner-toun to Dauvit's Roxburgh)
Juist doun the shank here in the Harecleuch Wuid
Blackadder sterts and eiks her watters til
The haill system, as does aw the laws we see
Contribute to this slaw syke wast to east,
And Twinlaw aye the perfect place to staund
And compass the haill swoup o't – jalouse
Tweed's rin ae time out ouer a German plain
To tak in Forth and syne fa tributar
To Rhine whase meikle delta geylikes fanned
Northlins throu tundra til the Baltic Minch

'Here Hutton, hatted farmer, stands
in Swallow Cleugh the height of summer ...'

Here Hutton with his hat off stands
in Swallow Cleugh the height of summer,
to contemplate, to question and to measure
in his mind one weak water's course through that –
that wide sinuous sine-curve in red sandstone,
deep-cut cleft through Berwick's richest rock ...
and gradually his speculative insect's mind
for fine-tuned reading of the land has sensed
the river's slowly alternating beat
from one bank to the other.

And the long relentless wear.

He matches rock's course against water's,
weighs the rock's course with the water's
and he finds
on the blind-fool Christian's plain redundant tron
the balance wanting.
What makes up the measure?

Time. Time, simple.
Time alone.

Time in great quantity ...

all the many languages
of berwickshire
all the many tributaries
its two chief rivers
flowing into tweed
all the many
all the many
melting into one
cairn stone silence
presences
high
presences
bleak
on barren hills
between
blood's
rock-worn runnels

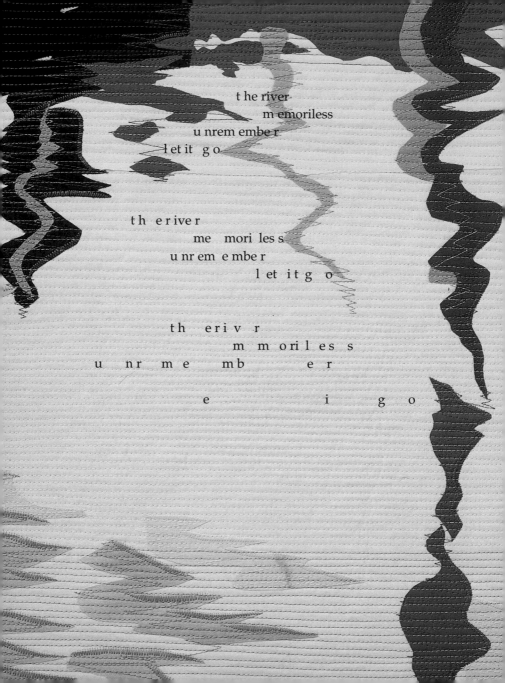

the river
memoriless
unremember
let it go

th e river
me mori les s
u nr em e mbe r
l et it g o

th erivr
m mori les s
u nr me mb er
e i go

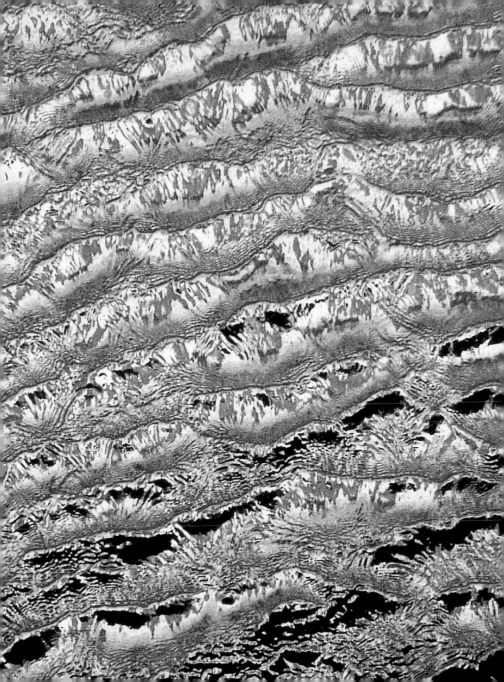

For the Pearl Fishers

Words and Graphics **Alec Finlay**

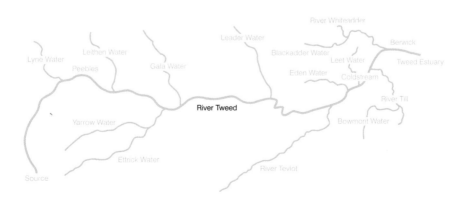

A single river pearl, fished from the River Laxford in Sutherland in 1992 by Eddie Davies, has been returned to the River Tweed, somewhere between its source and the sea. The pearl is soft mauve-pink on top and dark brown underneath.

River   **Tweed Estuary**

Images   Judy Thomas

Notes

Cover:

The Gateheugh is a rocky cliff below Scott's View, near Dryburgh. It lies opposite the site of Old Melrose monastery, where St Cuthbert was a monk.

Tweed:

A glossary of Scots and Northumbrian words used in the three sections of the poem.

Bob Morrison (p. 166)	*a traditional name for the grey heron among Tillmouth salmon netsmen*
Caa' (p. 85)	*eddy*
Cairn net (p. 86)	*net anchored by a heap of stones*
Cauld (p. 85)	*weir*
Claed (p. 86)	*clothed*
Cleek (p. 86)	*to catch salmon using stick and hook*
Drumly (p. 165)	*clouded*
Glaur (p. 25)	*sticky mud*
Guddle (p. 86)	*to catch salmon by hand*
Gump (p. 86)	*same as 'guddle'*
Haad your wheesht (p. 85)	*be quiet*
Harl (p. 89)	*barb or filament*
Haugh (p. 167)	*flat, boggy ground*
Jeannies (p. 85)	*spinning machines*
Jock Scott (p. 89)	*this and the other names in this passage are all types of salmon or trout fly*
Keel (p. 25)	*ruddle*
Lade (p. 85)	*watercourse*
Linn (p. 29)	*waterfall*
Point (p. 166)	*the peak moment when the incoming tide reaches the netting station*
Rashers (p. 25)	*rushes*
Rouk (p. 166)	*river mist*
Shoon (p. 86)	*shoes*
Sneggle (p. 86)	*to catch salmon by foul-hooking*
Tacketty boots (p. 25)	*hobnail boots*
Tows (p. 169)	*ropes*
Woomlick (p. 169)	*hemlock and similar, such as hogweed*

Lyne Water:

p. 45 Enomoto Kikaku (1661–1707) was a Japanese haiku poet.

p. 46 'Matritamah' is one of 108 names of the Ganges recited on a Ganga Dhaaraa, which is a *teerath* or pilgrimage.

Leader Water:

p. 114 The lines by Eavan Boland come from 'Anna Liffey', in *Collected Poems* (Carcanet Press, 1995).

p. 114 'The Dass': 'dass' is a Scots word for a ledge on a hillside or cliff. That referred to here is the name of a particular spot near Longmoormoss.

p. 116 The quoted text by Edith Hope is taken from *Bondagers* by Ian Macdougall (Tuckwell, 1995).

p. 119 The quote beginning 'It is maintained . . .' is taken from *Lauder and Lauderdale* by A. Thomson (1902; reprint, Galashiels: Sykes Europe Ltd., 2001).

p. 121 The quote about the Great Flood of 1948 is taken from *Lauderdale in the Twentieth Century*, edited by Norrie McLeish and Fay Mackay (2002).

p. 127 'Sugarlift' and 'aquatint' are techniques used in intaglio printing, a process in which the image is either etched or engraved below the surface of the printing plate. 'Sugarlift' is a positive drawing technique involving a mix of sugar and Indian ink, while 'aquatint' is a way of adding different tones to the plate.

River Whiteadder and Blackadder Water:

p. 212 The lines in French are taken from Guillaume le Clerc's thirteenth century *Roman de Fergus*, and describe the Scotland-wide flight of a white stag from Perceval: 'the country of the Lammermuirs / it crosses also without let . . .'

p. 215 'Dauvit': David I (ruled 1124–53) saw the Merse not as a border but as the southern heartland in a kingdom that included Northumbria. Along with his abbey-building programme, urban development of the Roxburgh-Berwick nexus was a component part of his policy for the region. Failure of his successors to keep the region politically intact contributed to its ruinous instability in the later medieval and renaissance periods.

p. 216 James Hutton (1726–1797), author of *The Theory of the Earth* (1787), is considered the founder of the modern science of geology. In *The Man Who Found Time* (2003), Repcheck describes the thirteen years he spent in Berwickshire as 'unquestionably the most creative period of [his] life, comparable to Charles Darwin's five years aboard the Beagle', but fails to appreciate the range of geophysical features available to him in the immediate vicinity of Slighhouses, where he farmed from 1754 until 1767. Whiteadder's 'hidden' cleugh marks the southern perimeter to what was Hutton's land.

The textile works featured are: 'Wind-over-water' (pp. 207–209, 211–212); 'Dancing Lines' (pp. 218, 220); and 'Tweed Reflection II' (pp. 221–222). All photographs of the works are by Keith Tidball. The images on p. 210 and p. 219 are taken from digital photographs of Whiteadder Reservoir.

For the Pearl Fishers:

This was published as a postcard by Morning Star for the Tweed Rivers Interpretation Project in 2004.

Tweed Estuary:

The images were made in and around the walls of Berwick and the mouth of the Tweed. Pinhole cameras were made out of empty cider cans, which were loaded with lithographic film. There was no predicting what the outcome of these images would be. The cameras were left in various locations on several different occasions. The exposure times varied according to the weather conditions and time of day. The cameras were often disturbed, blown around or tampered with; all adding to the element of chance. The images have been kept as negatives to reflect this subverting of ordinary perception.

Biographies

Dorothy Alexander was born and brought up in Peebles and has lived all her life in the Scottish Borders. Her grandparents and father worked in the woollen mills in Innerleithen, and her grandfather and father were both enthusiastic trout-fishers. She won the Macallan / Scotland on Sunday Short Story Competition 2002, and recently completed an MLitt in Creative Writing at the University of Glasgow. She lives in Galashiels.

Birtley Aris was born in Sunderland in 1927, and lived in London and the south until 1962, when he returned to the north of England. He is a widely exhibited painter, who has also worked in stained glass. He has produced a series of paintings and drawings based on the poetry of Edward Thomas, William Morris and T.S. Eliot, and has collaborated with Linda France on several previous projects. He lives in Hexham.

John Behm is a painter and sculptor, with degrees in Fine and Applied Arts from Edinburgh College of Art. He conceived the *Waymerks* project for which small artworks in kists were hidden at locations along the Southern Upland Way, to be discovered by walkers. He lives within a few yards of the Whiteadder at Abbey St Bathans.

Gavin Bowd grew up in Galashiels. He is the author of poetry, fiction, translations and essays on Scottish and European literature and politics. He was the Founding Director of StAnza, the St Andrews poetry festival. He lectures in French at the University of St Andrews, and lives in Dundee.

Nigel Bridges was born in Hawick in 1958 and brought up near Jedburgh. He served for six years with the Royal Marines and saw active service in the Falklands. He later trained as a stockbroker before spending four years managing communications and information technology. Since 1989 he has worked as a cabinetmaker and artist-craftsman. He lives near Melrose.

Pauline Burbidge trained at St Martins Art College, London. She is a textile artist, making large-scale wall hangings inspired by water reflections. Her work has been exhibited throughout the UK, and in France, Japan and the USA. She lives at the confluence of the Blackadder and Whiteadder rivers.

Fred Cannon is a full-time artist. With his wife, Janet Rowntree Cannon, he presented the joint exhibition *The Ettrick Valley – An Illustrated Journey* at Halliwell's House Museum, Selkirk, in 2003, featuring work they had made during an intensive year's exploration of the area.

Colin Donati grew up in Roxburghshire, the son of a dairyman who moved his family between farms. A poet and musician, he writes in both English and Scots, and is currently completing a Scots version of Dostoyevsky's *Crime and Punishment*. He lives in Edinburgh.

Walter Elliot was born in Selkirk in 1934, spending his early life in Ettrick Valley and serving in The King's Own Scottish Borderers from 1952 to 1954, mainly in Northern Ireland. From 1954 to 1986 he worked in the fields and hills of the Borders as a fencer and woodcutter. A fractured skull caused a career change to museum assistant for four years. Though now retired, he writes, broadcasts and lectures on Borders history, archaeology, language and literature. He lives in Selkirk.

Alec Finlay is an artist, poet and publisher. The pocketbooks series (1998–2002), which he conceived and edited, proposed 'a contemporary generalist vision of Scottish culture'. He was publisher-in-residence at BALTIC The Centre for Contemporary Art, Gateshead, 2002–03, and now lives in Newcastle-upon-Tyne.

Linda France was born in 1958 in Newcastle-upon-Tyne. After living in Dorset, Leeds, London and Amsterdam, she returned to the North East in 1981, and now lives in Northumberland. She has two children and works as a freelance writer and part-time tutor in adult education. Her collections of poems include *Red* (1992), *Storyville* (1997) and *The Simultaneous Dress* (2002), and she is the editor of the anthology *Sixty Women Poets* (1993). She has collaborated with Birtley Aris on several previous projects.

Valerie Gillies is a poet and teacher who grew up in southern Scotland and studied in Edinburgh and Mysore, India. She has published seven collections of poetry including *Tweed Journey* (1989). In 2002 the Trimontium Trust appointed her, for life, *poeta vatesque sola trimontium* (sole poet and seer to Trimontium), probably the oldest laureateship in Britain. She received a Creative Scotland Award in 2005.

Earl Haig is a distinguished painter, whose landscapes in oil and watercolour are inspired by the countryside around Bemersyde, the family home close to Newtown St Boswells and the River Tweed, where he has lived since 1924.

Rob Hain graduated in Fine Art from Loughborough College of Art and Design in 1977. He began to paint professionally in 1981, the same year as he settled in the Scottish Borders with his wife, the painter Margaret Scott. His work includes a ceiling mural commissioned by The Italian Centre in Glasgow, which received a Civic Trust Award, and he has been artist-in-residence at the Tweed Festival. He lives near Melrose.

Susheila Jamieson was born and brought up Dundee. After studying Psychology at the University of St Andrews, she worked abroad for several years before returning to Scotland and graduating in Sculpture from Edinburgh College of Art. As a sculptor she works in hardwood or stone, and has been commissioned to make work in France, and for various locations in Scotland. She lives near Biggar.

Mary Kenny is a professional artist, sculptor and storyteller living in Innerleithen. In 2000 she was commissioned to carve a series of stone panels tracing 2000 years of local history. These are sited at the Pirn iron-age hill fort, and the quill and ink drawings presented here are their companion piece.

Diane Lumley studied at Edinburgh College of Art, and later lectured at Duncan of Jordanstone College of Art, Dundee. She has exhibited and sold paintings through many Edinburgh galleries, and has worked as an illustrator for clients in the UK and North America. She lives in Melrose.

John McGregor is Edinburgh College of Art's photographer. His work has been widely published in newspapers and magazines, including *The Scotsman*, *The Times* and *Homes and Gardens*. With John Murray he fishes the Teviot near Kelso.

Alice Mitchell was born and brought up in England. She spent some years in Florence where she married an artist. In 1977 she and her four children moved to the Scottish Borders where she still lives. An English Literature graduate, she is a poet and storymaker.

John Murray is Head of the School of Landscape Architecture at Edinburgh College of Art. He has published two collections of poetry, *Aspen* (1996), and *Chiaroscuro* (2001). He lives in Kelso.

Tom Murray lives in Selkirk. His stories and poems have been widely published in literary magazines in the UK as well as in the USA and Canada. A number of his plays for both young people and adults have been performed at various venues including the Traverse Theatre, Edinburgh. He is currently co-editor of the literary magazine *The Eildon Tree*.

Katrina Porteous is a poet, historian and broadcaster of Scottish origin who lives on the Northumberland coast. Her publications include *The Lost Music* (poems, 1996), *The Wund an' the Wetter* (book and CD, with Chris Ormston, 1999), *Turning the Tide* (2001), a collaboration with two artists on the restoration of the black beaches of east Durham, and *The Bonny Fisher Lad* (2003), a collection of reminiscences from inhabitants of Northumberland fishing villages. She has also written long landscape poems for broadcast on BBC Radio 3, 4 and Scotland.

Robert Quilietti has lived in the Scottish Borders for 25 years. He is well known as a children's entertainer and magician. More recently he has become known as a writer of short stories and plays, and his story 'The Ball' won Radio 4's Front Row competition. He lives in Berwickshire.

John Rogers paints in oils, watercolour and acrylics. He also produces small editions of wood engravings and stone lithographs. He lives in Peebles.

Judith Rowan studied at Leith School of Art and Cumbria College of Art and Design. Her work has been widely exhibited throughout Britain, and she was one of twelve women artists from Scotland and France who contributed to *Signs of the Zodiac*, a print project and book exhibited in both countries. She lived in the Scottish Borders for many years before moving to Edinburgh and then to her current home in East Lothian.

Judy Thomas worked as a youth and community tutor, and as an art teacher, before taking up a post in Education and Public Programme at BALTIC The Centre for Contemporary Art, Gateshead, in 2002. She is currently working towards a MA in Fine Art and Education at the University of Northumbria. She lives in Newcastle-upon-Tyne.

Site List

These are the sites where the Tweed Rivers Interpretation Project has provided interpretative material, or supported the work of community-based projects. All are informal sites, with no entrance charge. At a small number of sites work is due to be completed in summer 2005.

Tweed's Well
The source of the Tweed, on the A701 north of Moffat. Sculpture by Fly Freeman, installed in 1998.

Glentress Forest, near Peebles
Iron Age hill fort and reproduction of a roundhouse at Janet's Brae.

The Pirn, Innerleithen
An Iron Age hill fort, access from the B709. Sculptures by Mary Kenny.

St Mary's Loch
A sculpture by Matt Baker is on the south shore, a short walk along the Southern Upland Way. Dryhope Tower, near the east end of the loch, is a dramatic and well preserved example of a reiver's stronghold. At Henderland Bank, on the road to Megget reservoir, a medieval tomb nestles in a small wood.

Thornielee Forest, between Galashiels and Walkerburn
Sculpture by Rob Taylor.

Stow Bridge, Stow
An unusual pack-horse bridge, one of the oldest in the Borders.

Salmon Leap Walk, Selkirk
A route following the River Ettrick from Victoria Park to a cauld (a weir) where salmon jump upstream.

Lindean Loch
A local nature reserve near Selkirk.

Rhymers Stone, near Melrose
Where Thomas the Rhymer is said to have met the Queen of the Faeries.

Leaderfoot Viaduct, near Melrose
Just off the A68. Sculpture by Garry Fay; poetry by Valerie Gillies.

Scott's View
On the B6356 near St Boswells.

Wallace's Statue, near Scott's View
Scotland's first memorial to William Wallace, commissioned by the Earl of Buchan in 1814.

The Temple of the Muses, near Dryburgh

A monument to the poet James Thomson, also commissioned by the Earl of Buchan.
Sculpture by Siobhan O'Hehir.

Crystal Well

On the banks of the Tweed below Benrig Cemetery, near St Boswells.

The Junction Pool, Maxwellheugh Viewpoint, and Belmont Brae, Kelso

The Junction Pool is at the meeting of the Teviot and the Tweed, and one of the most famous fishing pools
in the world. Sculpture by Rob Taylor. Maxwellheugh Viewpoint is on the Jedburgh road; Belmont Brae
overlooks the site of the original bridge across the Tweed.

Roxburgh Castle and medieval burgh

Along the River Teviot near Kelso.

Cessford Castle, near Morebattle

The impressive ruins of a heavily fortified house, built by ancestors of the Duke of Roxburgh.

Pennymuir Roman Camps, near Morebattle

Some of the best preserved Roman marching camps in Scotland.

Hawick Mote

A Norman motte and bailey on the south edge of the town. Seating and railings by Denys Mitchell;
artwork by local schoolchildren and Irene Beston.

Inchbonny, Jedburgh

James Hutton developed his 'theory of the earth', the foundation of modern geology, from observations
of rock formations to the south of the town. Interpretation includes a sculpture by Max Nowell.

Henderson Park, Coldstream

Railings by Denys Mitchell, poetry by Valerie Gillies.

Union Bridge

Four miles west of Berwick-upon-Tweed; Europe's oldest road suspension bridge (1819–20) is still in use.

Paxton House, near Berwick-upon-Tweed

An attractive walk along the Tweed runs through the grounds.

Berwick-upon-Tweed

Trails around Castlegate, a sculpture by Jim Whitson overlooking the Tweed, and a paddling pool in
Spittal by Kay Ridley and local schoolchildren.

BERWICK

Whiteadder Water

HallBroch

Union Suspension Bridge

COLDSTREAM

Leet Water

Twizel

Water

ELSO

River Till

Flodden

Princes feather

Coal foot

Cheeper

Sheep Rot

with the duelle

Here my trouthe j will the plygte ...

Index of Contributors